THE UNOFFICIAL AEROPRESS COFFEE MAKER

RECIPE BOOK

101 Barista-Quality Coffee & Espresso Drinks You Can Make At Home

By Mike Alan

healthy happy Foodie

HHF Press
San Francisco

COPYRIGHT © 2020 Healthy Happy Foodie Press (HHF Press)

First published 2020

All rights reserved. No part of this book may be reproduced in any form or by any electronic or mechanical means, including information storage and retrieval systems, without permission in writing from the publisher, except by reviewers, who may quote brief passages in a review.

Editor: HHF Press

Art Direction: HHF Press

Illustrations: HHF Press

All photographs in this book © HHF Press, © Shutterstock.com or © Depositphotos.com

Published in the United States of America by HHF Press

268 Bush St, #3042

San Francisco, CA 94104 USA

www.HHFPress.com

Disclaimer:

Although the publisher and authors of this book are practically obsessed with modern cooking techniques, neither the publisher nor the authors represent or are affiliated with any of the brands mentioned in this text.

All content herein represents the authors' own experiences and opinions, and do not represent medical or health advice. The responsibility for the consequences of your actions, including your use or misuse of any suggestion or procedure described in this book lies not with the authors, publisher or distributors of this book. We recommend using common sense and consulting with a licensed health professional before changing your diet or exercise. The authors or the publisher do not assume any liability for the use of or inability to use any or all of the information contained in this book, nor do the authors or publisher accept responsibility for any type of loss or damage that may be experienced by the user as the result of activities occurring from the use of any information in this book. Use the information responsibly and at your own risk.

The authors and publisher reserve the right to make changes he or she deems required to future versions of the publication to maintain accuracy.

CONTENTS

WHY YOU NEED THIS BOOK!	1
WHY USE THE AEROPRESS	5
THE SURPRISING HEALTH BENEFITS OF AEROPRESS COFFEE	9
HOW TO USE THE AEROPRESS	12
PRO TIPS TO MAKE PERFECT AEROPRESS COFFEE AND OTHER CONCOCTIONS	17
GRIND GUIDE: HOW TO GET THE MOST OUT OF YOUR BEANS	21
ESPRESSO COFFEE RECIPES	26
Almond Espresso Ice Cream Float	27
Black Russian Espresso	28
Chilled Espresso Martini	29
Espresso Royal	30
Hot Buttered Chocolate-Caramel Espresso	31
Lassi Style Espresso	32
Peppermint Espresso Cream	33
Perfect Iced Espresso	34
Sicilian Espresso Martini	35
Tangy Bourbon Espresso	36
Walnut Espresso Frappe	37
LATTE COFFEE RECIPES	38
Almond Milk Cold Brew Latte	39
Amaretto Almond Latte	40
Cinnamon Dolce Latte	41
Creamy Eggnog Latte	42
Creamy Italian Coffee	43
Gingerbread Latte	44
Gingerbread Latte Supreme	45
Almond Coffee	46
Hot Buttered Coffee	47
Maple Cream Latte	48
Marshmallow Cream Latte	49

Nutella Blended Latte	50
Orange Mocha Latte	51
Tembleque Latte	52
Vanilla Ginger Latte	53
White Chocolate Latte	54

CAPPUCCINOS — 55

Authentic Cappuccino	56
Black Forest Cappuccino	57
Cinnamon Mocha Cappuccino	58
Hazelnut Cappuccino	59
Iced Eggnog Cappuccino	60
Mocha Mint Cappuccino	61

CHOCOLATE CARAMEL COFFEES — 62

Amaretto and Chocolate Coffee	63
Black Magic Chocolate Coffee	64
Brown Sugar Caramel Latte	65
Caramel Macchiato	66
Homemade Vanilla Syrup	67
Chocolate and Vanilla Latte	68
Mayan Coffee	69
Viennese Coffee	70
Whipped Chocolate and Vanilla Mocha	71

MOCHA COFFEES — 72

Caramel Cream Mocha	73
Easy Cinnamon Mocha Latte	74
Hot Cocoa Mocha Latte	75
Mint Mocha Latte	76
Peanut Butter Mocha	77
Peppermint Mocha	78
Salted Caramel Mocha Frappuccino	79
Simple Cafe Mocha	80

FRUITY AND SPICED COFFEES — 81

Banana Coconut Coffee Frappe	82
Berry Mocha	83
Blueberry White Chocolate Latte	84

Chocolate-Cherry Frappe	85
Coconut Oil Coffee	86
Honey Coffee	87
Raspberry Frappe	88
Cold Brew	89
Strawberry Iced Coffee	90

ICED COFFEES   91

Blended Iced Espresso	92
Caribbean Spiced Coffee Soda	93
Chocolate-Cinnamon Iced Cappuccino	94
Coconut Mocha Iced Coffee	95
Coffee Ice Cubes	96
Cold Brewed Horchata Coffee	97
Cold Brewed Iced Mocha	98
Cold Brewed Vanilla Caramel Coffee	99
Frozen Caramel-Cinnamon Latte	100
Hazelnut Mocha Smoothie	101
Honey Cinnamon Iced Coffee	102
Iced Coconut Latte	103
Old Fashioned Coffee Soda	104
Simple Coffee Frappe	105
Simple Cold Brewed Coffee	106

INTERNATIONAL COFFEES   107

African Coffee Punch	108
Authentic Irish Coffee	109
Brazilian Coffee	110
Brazilian Coffee Soda	111
Cuban Iced Coffee	112
Dublin Iced Coffee	113
Guatemalan Hop	114
Irish Cappuccino	115
Mexican Espresso	116
Spicy Thai Iced Coffee	117
Thai Coffee	118
The World's Best Pumpkin Spice Latte	119
Traditional Turkish Coffee	120

Vietnamese Coffee	121
Warm Gingerbread Irish Coffee	122

COFFEE COCKTAILS — 123

Cafe Imperial	124
Cafe Rumba	125
Chocolate Stout Affogato	126
Coffee Liqueur	127
Creamy Cinnamon Coffee Punch	128
Creamy Spiked Coffee	129
Spiced Coffee Cocktail	130
Summer Espresso Gin Fizz	131
Irish Coffee	132
The Dude	133
Warm Strawberry Vanilla Espresso Cocktail	134

BONUS — 135

The Perfect Aeropress Tiramisu	137
Aeropress Espresso Cheesecake	138

CHAPTER 1
Why You Need This Book!

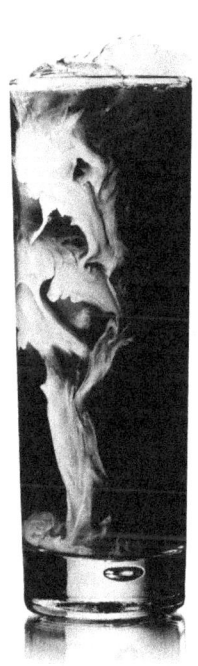

It's The ONLY Book Written Specifically for The Aeropress!

There are many books out there that will teach you tips for brewing the perfect cup of coffee, but this is the first and only book that will teach you how to become an expert barista using the Aeropress coffee maker. As you may already be aware, the Aeropress is a revolutionary coffee making system that is designed to make the perfect cup of coffee for all tastes. From traditional drip-style coffee to exotic espresso drinks, the Aeropress' outperforms any at-home brewing system, and because it is so simple to use, you can become an expert in no time. This book will cover everything you need to know to get the most out of your Aeropress coffee maker, including recipes, techniques, and tips to make the absolute best cup of coffee you've ever tasted.

Unlock Your Aeropress' Potential for Amazing Coffee Drinks

The perfect cup of coffee...It sounds so simple, but as any coffee aficionado can tell you, the perfect cup can be hard to come by—especially at home. For years now, the standard for brewing a cup of strong coffee has been the French press. The Aeropress takes the concept of the French press and brings it into the 21st century. By improving the main components of coffee making, the Aeropress delivers a stronger, smoother cup of coffee without the bitterness that can occur with other types of coffee makers. Since the Aeropress is capable of brewing both American-style drip coffee as well as espresso, you have more options than with other machines and the results will be excellent every time. And because the Aeropress is designed to produce the most full-bodied flavor of any coffee maker, it stays rich and strong even when iced so there's no need for watery iced coffee ever again. We'll discuss all of the techniques you will need to tailor the perfect coffee to your tastes, and then explore styles and flavors for fun new coffee drinks.

Amazing Pro Tips for Making the Best Cup of Coffee You've Ever Had

Our helpful pro tips will turn you into an expert home barista in no time. Since the Aeropress is so versatile, you will learn tricks and tips to make many different styles of coffee by taking full advantage of what your Aeropress has to offer. Our industry-tested tips will show you how the pros get such perfectly balanced flavor from every cup, and because the Aeropress is so easy to use, you can use these tips to make the perfect cup of coffee in minutes. You will learn everything you need to know about brewing temperatures and times, how to customize your flavor, and get ideas to make your daily cup interesting and exciting. With the Aeropress, you never have to settle for a boring cup of coffee ever again.

Over 100 Delicious Recipes for Creative Coffee Drinks

Not only will this book teach you exactly how to use your Aeropress coffee maker, it will also provide over 100 creative recipes for spicing up your daily coffee. Professional baristas are always creating new ways of adding flavor to coffee, and now so can you. Our recipes will show you how to combine different flavors and techniques to exciting coffee every day of the week.

It's The ONLY Coffee Recipe Book You'll Ever Need

Not only does this book offer amazing recipes and the science behind the perfect cup of coffee, it will show you how to use your Aeropress to make the perfect cup of coffee consistently. The pros use fancy equipment to make delicious coffee, but thanks to the Aeropress, you can make the same drinks that the pros make, in your own home. And because the Aeropress is compact and easy to clean, you'll be able to take the Aeropress with you to make perfect coffee on the go!

CHAPTER 2
Why Use The Aeropress

The Aeropress Is the Absolute Best Way to Make Coffee

If you're a coffee lover, chances are you're always in search of the best method for brewing coffee. Thanks to the Aeropress, your search is over. If you've been using a French press, the Aeropress will seem familiar except for the fact that your coffee will come out tasting richer and smoother without the bitterness that can often result from French press brewing. And since the Aeropress is so versatile, you will be able to customize exactly how strong you want your coffee to be, and you can adjust this for each cup that you brew. Because of the Aeropress' patented micro filter, you will also avoid the grit that is found in many cups of coffee that can lead to an unpleasant aftertaste.

Learn Different Techniques for Creating Bold Flavors

The Aeropress specializes in making concentrated coffee that can be used for many different applications from traditional drip coffee to espresso. We're going to cover the basics of how to use the Aeropress, but we will also discuss the techniques that you can use to adjust the flavor and acidity level of your coffee and how to pair the coffee you brew with exciting flavors to keep your daily cup interesting. We'll also discuss how the grind of your beans affects strength and flavor, as well as learning which types of beans offer different flavor profiles.

It's The Most Convenient Way of Making Perfectly Brewed Coffee

The Aeropress is easy to use and clean and also makes perfect coffee every time. Since the process only requires a few seconds to brew, it will save you time every day. The Aeropress' revolutionary design takes all of the guesswork and mess out of brewing coffee and unlike pod-style machines, it produces fresh tasting coffee and doesn't cause unnecessary plastic waste. Simply decide which type of coffee you want, pour in the water and ground coffee, press the plunger and your coffee is made instantly.

It's The Most Durable Coffee Maker on The Market

The Aeropress is a simple yet highly advanced coffee making system that also offers the highest durability of any coffee maker on the market. Its components come apart easily for cleaning and are all made of high strength, non-BPA plastic. This means that you never need to worry about parts being dropped or breaking while cleaning. In fact, the Aeropress is so durable, it even comes with a nylon carrying bag so you can take it with you wherever you go. Imagine going camping and having perfectly brewed coffee around the campfire. Since the Aeropress is almost indestructible you can confidently carry it anywhere.

Cleaning the Aeropress is Easy and Fast!

Since the Aeropress is designed to be the world's easiest coffee maker, it is also designed to be the easiest to clean. Simply take the Aeropress apart and rinse with warm water. The used grounds are easy to eject straight into the trash, and you can even pop it in the dishwasher if desired. The Aeropress filters can be used multiple times with just a quick rinse between uses so you can be confident that you are being as green as possible while making the best coffee you've ever had.

CHAPTER 3
The Surprising Health Benefits of Aeropress Coffee

The Aeropress is The Best for Preserving Coffee's Essential Nutrients

Coffee has many health benefits, but one of the most important is the essential nutrients that coffee can provide. These nutrients include a full component of B vitamins. By brewing coffee without passing along harmful acids, these important B vitamins remain intact throughout the brewing process. One of the reasons the Aeropress produces such a great cup of coffee is that it doesn't use boiling water which can create bitterness, but it also means that the nutrients in the beans aren't affected by such high temperatures.

The Aeropress Unlocks Many Beneficial Anti-Oxidants

Did you know that Americans get more anti-oxidants from coffee than any other food? It's true. Coffee is an excellent source of vital anti-oxidants that help protect against heart disease and cancer. By neutralizing free radicals that exist throughout the body, anti-oxidants protect cells from many different threats. Because the Aeropress employs such a simple method for making coffee, these anti-oxidants are abundant in every cup of Aeropress coffee you drink.

Improve Your Energy and Attention with Aeropress Coffee

Most of us know that one of the main benefits of coffee is that it gives you a boost to start your day. What you may not know is that the energy enhancing benefits of coffee go beyond a jolt of caffeine. The caffeine in coffee triggers a response in your brain that inhibits certain neurotransmitters while allowing others, like dopamine, to become enhanced. This leads to an increase in the firing of neurons which makes you more alert and productive. Because the Aeropress system produces a concentrated coffee, you can tailor your caffeine level to your taste by adding water or other liquids to achieve your desired caffeine level. Never again have bland coffee because you were forced to add too much milk. The Aeropress allows you to have a rich flavorful cup at any caffeine level.

Coffee may Help You Burn Fat!

Numerous studies have shown that the amount of fat we burn is based, partly, on our metabolism. The faster our metabolism, the faster we burn fat. Coffee has been shown to boost metabolism in a more significant way than almost any other substance. In many people, the increase can be anywhere from 10%-30% which is enough to significantly improve your ability to burn excess fat. This combined with the fact that coffee is a safe and natural stimulant means that you are improving your metabolism while giving you the energy you need to tackle a tough workout.

Help Prevent Dementia and Parkinson's

Dementia is a problem that affects many older people and unfortunately, there is no cure. However, there are things that we can do to prevent these devastating diseases. The National Institutes of Health states that coffee has been shown to lower the risk of dementia disorders such as Alzheimer's and Parkinson's disease. Researchers are finding that lifetime coffee drinkers are at the lowest risk of developing these conditions later in life and coffee may reduce the risk by as much as 20%.
(https://www.ncbi.nlm.nih.gov/pubmed/20182054).

CHAPTER 4
How to Use the Aeropress

Setting Up Your Aeropress

One of the reasons that the Aeropress is becoming so popular among coffee lovers is that it is incredibly easy to use. Setting up the Aeropress is as easy as placing a micro filter into the chamber and placing the chamber on top of a sturdy mug. That's right, the Aeropress brews your coffee directly into your mug with no mess. Now it's time to brew.

How to Brew the Perfect Cup of Coffee in No Time!

Ok, so you've got your Aeropress set up. Let's brew a cup of coffee. Simply pour two scoops of coffee grounds into the chamber using the scoop that came with your Aeropress. It is recommended that you use water that is 175 degrees for the best tasting cup of coffee. Any higher and you may detect some bitterness, and any lower may result in weak coffee. Pour the water into the chamber and stir with the included paddle. Insert the plunger into the chamber and press down about a quarter of an inch. Hold the plunger in place for 20 to 30 seconds. As you press down on the plunger, the coffee will immediately begin dripping into the mug. Once the mug is full, you're finished.

1) Insert Filter:

2) Add Coffee / Water:

Hot (175°) or Cold

3) Use Plunger to Press Coffee:

 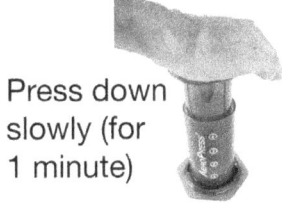

Press down slowly (for 1 minute)

How to Use the Aeropress' Unique Inversion Method

Another way of brewing with the Aeropress is known as the inversion method. This method produces a smoother, milder brew than the traditional Aeropress method. To do this, press the plunger about one and a half inches into the main chamber. Invert the Aeropress and place on counter so that the opening is facing you. Pour the freshly ground coffee into the chamber and slowly pour the hot water to the halfway point. Stir about a dozen times and fill the water to the top. Wet a filter and place it in the cap, then twist the cap on. Place your mug upside down on the Aeropress and carefully invert the Aeropress right-side up. Then press the plunger. You will find that it is easier to press down compared to the traditional method because there is less air inside the chamber creating resistance. Because the coffee grounds have longer to steep using this method, the resulting coffee will be a similar strength to traditional drip coffee, but it will taste much better.

Use The Aeropress to Make Amazing Iced Coffee

If you use the traditional method for brewing with the Aeropress, you will make amazing high concentration coffee quickly and easily, and this type of coffee is perfect for making a refreshing iced coffee. The problem with most iced coffee is, well, the ice. Since the ice begins melting immediately, you quickly wind up with watery tasting iced coffee instead of full flavored, robust coffee. Because the Aeropress produces a stronger, richer coffee, it will still taste strong with a little ice added to it. And because you can use your Aeropress to cold brew as well, you can have amazingly flavorful cold brewed coffee in as little as 20 minutes and skip the ice entirely.

How to Make Café Quality Espresso at Home with The Aeropress

The Aeropress is unique because it is the simplest system on the market and yet it can make espresso rival your favorite upscale coffee shop. Because the Aeropress is designed to produce a concentrated brew without any bitterness or excess acidity, you can easily achieve a dark espresso by simply substituting your usual coffee grounds with ground espresso beans. As with any brew, the strength of the coffee will be determined by the ratio of coffee grounds to water. You can experiment to find your ideal ratio, but making delicious espresso really is as easy as filling the Aeropress, stirring, and pressing the plunger. You can even add milk directly into the brewing process to create lattes or cappuccinos.

CHAPTER 5
Pro Tips to Make Perfect Aeropress Coffee and Other Concoctions

Make Coffee That is The Perfect Strength for You

The Aeropress makes coffee that, unlike traditional drip or French press methods, is designed to be diluted with water or milk. If you've ever made French press coffee that is too strong, you know that adding some water seriously diminishes the flavor. However, the Aeropress allows you to add water to concentrated coffee and still hold onto the rich, full flavor. Basically, the perfect Americano. The other problem with watering down traditional coffee is that traditional coffee is far more acidic than Aeropress coffee and the stronger the brew, the more acid. Watering down very acidic coffee won't get rid of that bitter flavor, but thanks to the low acidity achieved by the Aeropress, you will never find yourself with a watery, bitter cup of coffee. Simply add as much water or milk as you want in order to reach the perfect strength. It's really that easy.

How to Use the Plunger Effectively

The only moving part of the entire Aeropress system is the plunger. The plunger creates pressure within the chamber and allows the coffee to gently infuse into the water. The best method for using the plunger is steady, and gentle pressure. There is no need to press down too hard, and even with gentle pressure, a cup of coffee should only take about a minute to produce. In order to get the most out of every brew, be sure to press the plunger down completely, that way the rubber plunger re-expands to its full size, which helps it stay airtight to allow the air to be pushed through, giving you some crema which you will notice is the light brown foam found on the top of a well-made cup of espresso.

Spice Up Your Daily Coffee with Exotic Flavors

Coffee is a part of many people's everyday routine, but that doesn't mean that has to be the same cup of coffee every day. In our recipe section, we're going to discuss how you can use spices and other flavors to create interesting and flavorful coffee drinks that will make every morning a new adventure. The reason the Aeropress is so well suited to making flavored coffees is because its micro filter system allows you to add powdered spices to the brewing coffee so that it infuses into the coffee but doesn't show up in your cup. You get all of the flavor and none of the grit that often results from other brewing methods.

The Right Amount of Water Makes All the Difference

When choosing what kind of coffee you want to make, the most important questions are, how much coffee should I use, and how much water should I use? Luckily, the Aeropress takes the guess work out of this by making each cup individually. About eight ounces of water is all you need to make a rich cup of coffee that you can then dilute with water or milk to suit your taste. Or skip the water and milk altogether and enjoy a rich cup of espresso that tastes like it came from an expensive coffee shop.

The Best Way to Store Your Aeropress

Because the Aeropress is so durable, storage couldn't be easier. Unlike fragile brewing systems like the French press, the Aeropress can be stored anywhere without worrying about breakage. To clean and store the Aeropress, simply remove the cap, push the plunger to eject the used coffee, and rinse the rubber seal. The Aeropress is practically self-cleaning, but it can also be washed in the dishwasher. To make it compact, you will store the plunger inside the chamber. For added convenience as well as perfectly brewed coffee on the go, a nylon tote bag is available to store the Aeropress. This makes the Aeropress perfect for camping or traveling.

CHAPTER 6
Grind Guide: How to Get the Most Out of Your Beans

The Aeropress Works with All Types of Coffee

From traditional roasts to exotic espressos, the Aeropress can handle whatever you want to brew. More traditional systems like the French press are limited because you are forced to use a certain grind in order to make coffee. Use a grind that is too fine with a French press and you will end up with a gritty, bitter sludge. Thankfully, the Aeropress uses a micro filter system that allows you to use whatever type of grind you prefer. If you like the nuance and strength of a very fine grind, you can make that without ever worrying that the grounds will end up in the cup. And if you prefer a coarser grind, you never have to worry about making a weak cup of coffee because the Aeropress infuses the coffee into the water so completely that every cup you brew will be full bodied and robust.

Regular Coffee vs. Espresso?

So what is the difference between regular coffee and espresso? Though the drinks may appear quite different, there isn't actually much of a difference between the raw materials. There is no such thing as an "espresso bean", and, in fact, espresso can be made from a variety of different types of coffee bean, and in some cases careful blends of different types. The big difference is the grind. Espresso is made from coffee beans that are ground much finer than standard ground coffee. It is for this reason that most coffee makers are not suited to making espresso. If you've ever ground your coffee finer than usual and used it in a drip or French press system, you have likely experienced grit in your mug. Neither drip nor French press are designed to handle such a fine grind. The Aeropress, however, is perfect because of its unique micro filters. The filters are made of a material that allows you to use both coarse, medium, and fine espresso grinds without any grit finding its way into your coffee.

Fine Ground vs. Coarse Ground. Which is Right for You?

As mentioned above, the grind is what tends to determine the overall strength and character of your coffee. For a light black coffee many people prefer a coarse grind because it provides an easy to drink cup of coffee that doesn't require milk. Others prefer a much finer grind because not only it makes a stronger cup but also, it changes the texture of the coffee. Espresso has a thicker, almost creamy quality that is a product of a very fine grind. Of course, it's all a matter of preference, but however you like your coffee, the Aeropress will make the best cup you've ever made.

Choosing The Right Roast for Your Daily Coffee

Coffee beans get their signature flavor from several factors. Perhaps, the most important is how they are roasted. All coffee beans are roasted because if they weren't, they wouldn't taste like coffee at all. Light roasted beans are more acidic and contain more caffeine. Dark roasted beans are the other end of the spectrum, being less acidic and containing less caffeine. While lighter roasts tend to have a more assertive flavor, many people prefer the dark roast because it has a smoother, richer flavor. However, if you happen to like to taste the geographic origins of your beans, you might like a lighter roast; as the darker the beans are roasted, the more they lose their original flavor and take on the flavor of the roast.

Coffees of The World: The Difference Between Regions

Coffee beans are grown in warm climates all over the world, and there are some subtle differences in terms of flavor and strength. In the United States, the most common coffee is imported from Central America. These beans tend to be what we think of as normal coffee. They are well balanced and mix well with flavors and spices. South American coffee, most commonly Colombian coffee, is less acidic and more mellow flavored. African coffees, often originating in Kenya or Ethiopia tend to be bolder and have more of a fruity quality. This is partly due to the beans themselves and partially due to the way the beans are harvested and dried. Indonesian and Sumatran coffees are among the world's strongest and earthiest flavors. They tend to be roasted darker and because of this, have a smokier flavor than other coffees.

CHAPTER 7
Espresso Coffee Recipes

Almond Espresso Ice Cream Float

SERVINGS: 2 | PREP TIME: 20 MINUTES | COOK TIME: 5 MINUTES

This delicious cold brewed dessert coffee will wow your guests after a great meal, or can be enjoyed on a hot day.

INGREDIENTS:

- 1 tablespoon finely ground coffee
- 1 cup cold milk
- 2 tablespoons chocolate syrup
- 1/8 teaspoon almond extract or 1 tablespoon almond syrup
- 2 scoops coffee or espresso ice cream
- 1 can cream soda
- Whipped cream

INSTRUCTIONS:

1. Pour ground coffee, water, and almond extract into the Aeropress chamber and stir for about 10 seconds. Then allow to steep for 20 minutes, then press coffee.
2. Chill two tall glasses in the freezer and when they are cold, add one scoop of ice cream to each glass.
3. Pour the milk into the coffee and then pour the coffee over the ice cream.
4. Fill each glass with the cream soda and top each glass with one tablespoon of chocolate syrup. Top with whipped cream if desired.

Black Russian Espresso

SERVINGS: 2 | PREP TIME: 25 MINUTES | COOK TIME: 5 MINUTES

This espresso cocktail combines the rich strong flavor of Aeropress espresso with a traditional Black Russian for an elegant and decadent after dinner drink.

INGREDIENTS:

- 1 tablespoon finely ground coffee
- 1 cup cold water
- 2 ounces Kahlua coffee liqueur
- 2 ounces vodka
- Ice cubes

INSTRUCTIONS:

1. Pour the coffee and cold water into the Aeropress chamber and stir for about 10 seconds. Let steep for about 20 minutes, then press coffee.
2. In a cocktail shaker, combine the espresso, Kahlua, vodka, and ice. Shake well and strain into chilled martini glasses to serve.

Chilled Espresso Martini

SERVINGS: 2 | PREP TIME: 25 MINUTES | COOK TIME: 5 MINUTES

This elegant coffee cocktail is sure to be a hit at your next get together or whip up a batch any time and enjoy a classy way to have espresso.

INGREDIENTS:

- 1 tablespoon finely ground coffee
- 1 cup cold water
- 3 ounces vodka
- 2 ounces crème de cacao
- 3 ounces Kahlua
- Ice cubes

INSTRUCTIONS:

1. Pour the coffee and cold water into the Aeropress chamber and stir for about 10 seconds. Let steep for about 20 minutes, then press coffee.
2. Insert the plunger and press down gently for about 1 minute.
3. In a cocktail shaker, combine the coffee, vodka, Kahlua, and crème de cacao, and ice. Shake well and pour into chilled martini glasses.

Espresso Royal

SERVINGS: 2 | PREP TIME: 10 MINUTES | COOK TIME: 5 MINUTES

A sophisticated after dinner coffee that combines Cognac with the rich flavor of Aeropress coffee.

INGREDIENTS:

- 1 tablespoon finely ground coffee
- 1 cup water at 175F
- 4 ounces cognac or brandy
- 4 teaspoons sugar
- Whipped cream

INSTRUCTIONS:

1. Pour the coffee and hot water into the Aeropress chamber and stir for about 10 seconds, then press coffee.
2. In a small bowl, whip the cream so that it is very stiff.
3. Divide the espresso into two mugs and stir in the sugar and Cognac until the sugar is dissolved.
4. Top with whipped cream and serve immediately. Tip: To make this an Americano style drink, simply dilute the espresso with an additional cup of water.

Hot Buttered Chocolate-Caramel Espresso

SERVINGS: 2 | PREP TIME: 5 MINUTES | COOK TIME: 5 MINUTES

This flavorful dessert coffee combines strong coffee with sweet flavors to create a rich and balanced experience.

INGREDIENTS:

1 tablespoon finely ground coffee
1 cup water at 175F
1 teaspoon brown sugar
1 teaspoon butter
2 tablespoons chocolate syrup
2 ounces dark rum (optional)

INSTRUCTIONS:

1. Pour the ground coffee and hot water into the Aeropress chamber and stir for about 10 seconds, then press coffee.
2. In a small bowl stir together the sugar, butter, and chocolate syrup.
3. Divide the coffee into two mugs and stir half of the butter and sugar mixture into each cup. Stir until dissolved and serve.

Lassi Style Espresso

SERVINGS: 2 | PREP TIME: 5 MINUTES | COOK TIME: 5 MINUTES

This Middle Eastern inspired coffee is rich and smooth thanks to the addition of yogurt. The rich flavor of your Aeropress coffee balances well with the tangy yogurt flavor.

INGREDIENTS:

- 1 tablespoon finely ground coffee
- 1 cup water at 175F
- 1 cup plain or vanilla flavored yogurt
- 1/2 cup half and half or milk
- 2 tablespoons sugar
- Ice cubes

INSTRUCTIONS:

1. Pour the coffee and hot water into the Aeropress chamber and stir for about 10 seconds, then press coffee.
2. Fill two glasses with ice and spoon in the yogurt, half and half, and sugar.
3. Pour half of the espresso into each glass and stir well.

Peppermint Espresso Cream

SERVINGS: 2 | PREP TIME: 5 MINUTES | COOK TIME: 5 MINUTES

This simple espresso recipe packs a punch of peppermint while still allowing the flavor of your Aeropress coffee to shine through.

INGREDIENTS:

- 1 tablespoon finely ground coffee
- 1 cup water at 175F
- 1/2 teaspoon peppermint extract
- 4 tablespoons heavy cream or half and half

INSTRUCTIONS:

1. Pour the coffee and hot water into the Aeropress chamber and stir for about 10 seconds, then press coffee.
2. Divide the coffee into two mugs and add half of the peppermint extract to each cup.
3. Stir two tablespoons of heavy cream into each cup and serve.

Perfect Iced Espresso

SERVINGS: 2 | PREP TIME: 5 MINUTES | COOK TIME: 5 MINUTES

Espresso is an intense and rich drink that is full of complex flavors. Luckily, your Aeropress makes cafe quality espresso in minutes. This recipe will teach you how to make a basic espresso and what you can add to make it even more interesting.

INGREDIENTS:

2 tablespoons very finely ground coffee
1 cup water at 175F
Ice
2 tablespoons half and half (optional)
1 teaspoon sugar or agave syrup (optional)

INSTRUCTIONS:

1. Pour the ground coffee and hot water into the Aeropress chamber and stir for about 10 seconds. Allow to steep for another five minutes, then press coffee.
2. Since we're making iced espresso, place the concentrated coffee into the refrigerator for two hours.
3. Remove the coffee from the refrigerator and place ice in two glasses.
4. Pour the cold espresso over the ice and add one tablespoon of half and half to each glass.
5. If you prefer a milder drink, add a little more half and half. Finish with sugar if desired.

Sicilian Espresso Martini

SERVINGS: 2 | PREP TIME: 25 MINUTES | COOK TIME: 5 MINUTES

This sophisticated coffee martini hybrid is perfect for cocktail hour or after dinner.

INGREDIENTS:

- 1 tablespoon finely ground coffee
- 1 cup cold water
- 4 ounces sweet vermouth
- 3 ounces amaro
- 4 ounces sparkling water
- Ice cubes

INSTRUCTIONS:

1. Pour the coffee and cold water into the Aeropress chamber and stir for about 10 seconds. Let steep for about 20 minutes, then press coffee.
2. In a cocktail shaker, combine the coffee, vermouth, amaro, and ice. Shake well.
3. Pour into chilled martini glasses to serve.

Tangy Bourbon Espresso

SERVINGS: 4 | PREP TIME: 10 MINUTES | COOK TIME: 5 MINUTES

A truly complex espresso that combines citrus, spices, and bourbon for full robust flavors and lots of subtle undertones. Perfect for relaxing on a cold evening or for entertaining.

INGREDIENTS:

- 2 tablespoons finely ground coffee
- 2 cups water at 175F
- Zest of one orange
- 1 teaspoon ground cinnamon
- 1 teaspoon ground cardamom
- 1/2 teaspoon ground cloves
- 4 tablespoons sugar
- 4 tablespoons half and half
- 4 ounces bourbon

INSTRUCTIONS:

1. Pour the coffee, orange zest, cinnamon, cardamom, cloves, and half of the hot water, into the Aeropress chamber and stir for about 10 seconds, then press coffee.
2. Divide the espresso into four mugs and add one tablespoon of sugar, one ounce of bourbon and one tablespoon of half and half to each mug. Stir until the sugar is dissolved and serve.

Walnut Espresso Frappe

SERVINGS: 2 | PREP TIME: 10 MINUTES | COOK TIME: 5 MINUTES

This nutty dessert coffee has just the right blend of flavors thanks to earthy walnuts and natural vanilla.

INGREDIENTS:

1 tablespoon finely ground coffee
1 cup water at 175F
1/2 cup walnuts
1 tablespoon chocolate syrup
2 scoops vanilla ice cream
1 cup cold milk
1 teaspoon vanilla extract
Whipped cream (optional)

INSTRUCTIONS:

1. Pour the coffee and hot water into the Aeropress chamber and stir for about 10 seconds, then press coffee.
2. In a blender, combine the walnuts, chocolate syrup, milk, ice cream, vanilla extract, and coffee. Blend well and divide into two mugs.
3. Top with whipped cream if desired.

CHAPTER 8
Latte Coffee Recipes

Almond Milk Cold Brew Latte

SERVINGS: 4 | PREP TIME: 2 HOURS AND 20 MINUTES |
COOK TIME: 5 MINUTES

This is a fun way to present a coffee drink by first making espresso cubes and allowing them to slowly melt when the drink is served. It's simple and flavorful and easy to make.

INGREDIENTS:

- 2 tablespoons finely ground coffee
- 2 cups cold water
- 4 cups almond milk

INSTRUCTIONS:

1. Pour the coffee and half of the cold water into the Aeropress chamber and stir for about 10 seconds. Let steep for about 20 minutes, then press coffee.
2. Pour coffee into ice cube trays and place in the freezer for two hours.
3. When the coffee cubes are frozen, remove them from the freezer and divide them into four glasses.
4. Pour the almond milk over the coffee cubes and stir. As the cubes melt they will continue to add more and more flavor to the milk.

Amaretto Almond Latte

SERVINGS: 4 | PREP TIME: 10 MINUTES | COOK TIME: 5 MINUTES

This Italian inspired after dinner coffee is the perfect finish to any meal. And as always the bold flavor of your Aeropress coffee is the perfect base for any coffee drink.

INGREDIENTS:

- 2 tablespoons finely ground coffee
- 2 cups water at 175F
- 4 ounces Amaretto liqueur
- 1 tablespoon almond extract
- 2 cups steamed milk
- Whipped cream (optional)

INSTRUCTIONS:

1. Pour the coffee and half of the hot water into the Aeropress chamber and stir for about 10 seconds, then press coffee.
2. In a pitcher, combine the coffee, remaining water, Amaretto, and almond extract.
3. Steam the milk and stir into the pitcher with the coffee.
4. Divide the coffee into four mugs and serve topped with whipped cream.

Cinnamon Dolce Latte

SERVINGS: 2 | PREP TIME: 5 MINUTES | COOK TIME: 5 MINUTES

Try this simple recipe and spice up your regular latte with a little spice and a little sweetness. Add a little whipped cream and it becomes a delicious dessert coffee.

INGREDIENTS:

1 tablespoon finely ground coffee
1 cup water at 175F
1 cup frothed milk
2 tablespoons cinnamon syrup
Whipped cream (optional)
Ground cinnamon (optional)

INSTRUCTIONS:

1. Pour the coffee and hot water into the Aeropress chamber and stir for about 10 seconds, then press coffee.
2. In a small saucepan heat the milk and froth with a whisk or a hand steamer. Add the cinnamon syrup.
3. Divide the coffee evenly into two mugs. Add the steamed milk and top with whipped cream and a dash of ground cinnamon.
4. Tip: For a relaxing after dinner coffee, try adding one ounce of cognac or brandy.

Creamy Eggnog Latte

SERVINGS: 2 | PREP TIME: 5 MINUTES | COOK TIME: 5 MINUTES

This rich and creamy holiday favorite combines the assertive flavor of Aeropress coffee with lively spices like cinnamon and nutmeg.

INGREDIENTS:

- 1 tablespoon finely ground coffee
- 1 cup water at 175F
- 1/2 cup eggnog
- 1 cup frothed milk
- Cinnamon for topping

INSTRUCTIONS:

1. Pour the coffee and hot water into the Aeropress chamber and stir for about 10 seconds, then press coffee.
2. Divide the coffee into two mugs and add the half of the eggnog and milk to each mug.
3. Garnish with cinnamon to serve.

Creamy Italian Coffee

SERVINGS: 2 | PREP TIME: 5 MINUTES | COOK TIME: 5 MINUTES

This simple Italian coffee can be served hot or cold and is a great way to tweak your daily coffee with some flavorful spices.

INGREDIENTS:

- 1 tablespoon finely ground coffee
- 2 cups water at 175F
- 1 teaspoon cinnamon
- 1 teaspoon nutmeg
- 1 cup frothed milk
- 1 teaspoon sugar (optional)

INSTRUCTIONS:

1. Pour the coffee, one cup of hot water, cinnamon, and nutmeg into the Aeropress chamber and stir for about 10 seconds, then press coffee.
2. Divide the coffee into two mugs and dilute with the remaining water.
3. Add half of the milk to each mug and add sugar if desired.

Gingerbread Latte

SERVINGS: 4 | PREP TIME: 10 MINUTES | COOK TIME: 5 MINUTES

This coffee drink is perfect for entertaining around the holidays. The rich Aeropress coffee pairs perfectly with the sweets and spices that will remind you of home.

INGREDIENTS:

2 tablespoons finely ground coffee
2 cups water at 175F
2 cups steamed milk
1 tablespoon sugar
1 tablespoon gingerbread spice
Whipped cream (optional)

INSTRUCTIONS:

1. Pour the coffee, one cup of hot water, and gingerbread spice into the Aeropress chamber and stir for about 10 seconds, then press coffee.
2. Divide the coffee into 4 mugs and dilute with the remaining water. Then dilute further with the milk. Add the sugar and stir.
3. Serve with whipped cream if desired.

Gingerbread Latte Supreme

SERVINGS: 4 | PREP TIME: 20 MINUTES | COOK TIME: 10 MINUTES

This full flavored coffee drink combines lots of spices to create a complex and delicious drink that will awaken the senses and satisfy any taste. Perfect for a brisk autumn day.

INGREDIENTS:

- 2 tablespoons finely ground coffee
- 4 cups water at 175F
- 1/4 cup molasses
- 1/4 cup brown sugar
- 1 teaspoon ground ginger
- 1 teaspoon ground cinnamon
- 1 cup half and half
- 1 teaspoon ground cloves
- Whipped cream (optional)

INSTRUCTIONS:

1. In a bowl, combine the molasses, brown sugar, ginger, and cinnamon. Stir together and place in the refrigerator for 20 minutes
2. Pour coffee and half of the hot water into the Aeropress chamber and stir for about 10 seconds, then press coffee.
3. Dilute the coffee with the remaining water.
4. Add a tablespoon of the spice blend to each mug and then add the coffee and half and half. Stir well and served topped with whipped cream.
5. Hot Buttered

Almond Coffee

SERVINGS: 1 | PREP TIME: 5 MINUTES | COOK TIME: 5 MINUTES

This flavorful twist on buttered coffee adds a little almond extract while substituting actual butter for butter flavored powder. The result is a rich flavored drink that isn't as heavy as traditional buttered coffee.

INGREDIENTS:

- 1 tablespoon ground coffee
- 2 cups of water at 175F
- 1/2 teaspoon almond extract
- 1/2 teaspoon butter powder (Molly McButter or something similar)

INSTRUCTIONS:

1. Pour ground coffee and 1 cup of hot water into the chamber and stir for about 10 seconds, then press coffee.
2. Remove the Aeropress and dilute the coffee with the remaining water. Then add the butter powder and stir well.

Hot Buttered Coffee

SERVINGS: 2 | PREP TIME: 5 MINUTES | COOK TIME: 10 MINUTES

This trend is pretty recent, but hot buttered coffee is taking off because it is filling and allows caffeine to release more gradually for more sustained energy. It is also rich and frothy and tastes great.

INGREDIENTS:

2 tablespoons finely ground coffee
2 tablespoons unsalted butter
2 cups water at 175F
1 tablespoon sugar (optional if you like it a little sweeter)

INSTRUCTIONS:

1. Pour the ground coffee into the chamber and pour in the water.
2. Stir well for about 10 seconds and then allow to steep for about a minute, then press coffee.
3. Remove the Aeropress and pour the coffee into a blender or use a hand frothier to whip the coffee while adding the butter and sugar.
4. Once the coffee is nicely whipped, return it to the original mug to enjoy. It'll be the most satisfying cup you've had in a long time.
5. Tip: to make your buttered coffee even richer, try adding a teaspoon of coconut oil while blending.

Maple Cream Latte

SERVINGS: 2 | PREP TIME: 10 MINUTES | COOK TIME: 5 MINUTES

The flavor of pure maple syrup is infused in the milk for this rich and creamy latte that embodies the feelings of a brisk fall day in New England. For best results, use real A-grade maple syrup.

INGREDIENTS:

- 1 tablespoon finely ground coffee
- 1 cup water at 175F
- 1/4 cup pure maple syrup
- 1 cup whole milk
- Whipped cream (optional)

INSTRUCTIONS:

1. Pour the coffee and hot water into the Aeropress chamber and stir for about 10 seconds, then press coffee.
2. In a small saucepan, heat the milk and add the maple syrup over low heat. Stir well until all of the maple syrup has dissolved in the milk.
3. Pour in the coffee and stir well.
4. Divide into two mugs and top with whipped cream if desired.

Marshmallow Cream Latte

SERVINGS: 2 | PREP TIME: 5 MINUTES | COOK TIME: 5 MINUTES

This flavorful dessert coffee uses marshmallow fluff as an interesting way to sweeten coffee instead of using regular sugar.

INGREDIENTS:

- 1 tablespoon finely ground coffee
- 1 cup water at 175F
- 1/2 cup marshmallow fluff
- 1 cup frothed milk
- Whipped cream (optional)

INSTRUCTIONS:

1. Pour the coffee and hot water into the Aeropress chamber and stir for about 10 seconds, then press coffee.
2. Whip together the marshmallow fluff and the frothed milk.
3. Pour the milk mixture into the coffee and stir well. Top with whipped cream to serve.

Nutella Blended Latte

SERVINGS: 2 | PREP TIME: 20 MINUTES | COOK TIME: 5 MINUTES

Nutella is a delicious addition to many desserts and it can also be used to make a sweet nutty flavored blended latte.

INGREDIENTS:

- 1 tablespoon finely ground coffee
- 1 cup cold water
- 2 cups cold milk
- 1 teaspoon vanilla extract
- 4 tablespoons Nutella
- 2 cups ice
- Whipped cream (optional)

INSTRUCTIONS:

1. Pour the coffee and cold water into the Aeropress chamber and stir for about 10 seconds. Then let steep for about 20 minutes, then press coffee.
2. In a blender, combine the coffee, milk, vanilla extract, Nutella, and ice. Blend well and divide into two tall glasses. Top with whipped cream if desired.

# Orange Mocha Latte

SERVINGS: 2 | PREP TIME: 10 MINUTES | COOK TIME: 10 MINUTES

This fruity take on the traditional mocha latte blends the flavor of orange zest with robust espresso to create an unlikely and complex drink.

INGREDIENTS:

- 1 tablespoon finely ground coffee
- 1 cup of water at 175F
- 1 cup hot milk
- 2 tablespoons chocolate sauce
- 1 tablespoon orange zest
- 1 tablespoon sugar

INSTRUCTIONS:

1. Pour the coffee and hot water into the Aeropress chamber and stir for about 10 seconds, then press coffee.
2. In a small sauce pan, heat the milk, sugar, and orange zest until it becomes frothy.
3. Divide the coffee into two mugs and pour half of the milk into each much.

Tembleque Latte

SERVINGS: 2 | PREP TIME: 5 MINUTES | COOK TIME: 5 MINUTES

This coconut infused latte can be served hot or cold depending on your mood, but thanks to your Aeropress, it will be rich and flavorful either way.

INGREDIENTS:

- 1 tablespoon finely ground coffee
- 1 cup water at 175F
- 1 cup warm milk
- 2 ounces coconut syrup
- 1 teaspoon ground cinnamon

INSTRUCTIONS:

1. Pour the coffee, hot water, and ground cinnamon into the Aeropress chamber and stir for about 10 seconds, then press coffee.
2. In a small sauce pan, warm the milk, but do not let it come to a boil. Add the coconut syrup and stir well.
3. Divide the coffee into two mugs and pour in the milk. Stir well and serve.

Vanilla Ginger Latte

SERVINGS: 2 | PREP TIME: 5 MINUTES | COOK TIME: 5 MINUTES

INGREDIENTS:

1 tablespoon coffee, finely ground
1 cup water at 175F
1 teaspoon finely chopped candied ginger
1/2 cup half and half, frothed
1/4 teaspoon vanilla extract

INSTRUCTIONS:

1. Pour coffee, hot water, candied ginger, and vanilla extract into the Aeropress chamber and stir for about 10 seconds, then press coffee.
2. Divide the coffee into two mugs and stir in the frothed half and half.

White Chocolate Latte

SERVINGS: 2 | PREP TIME: 10 MINUTES | COOK TIME: 5 MINUTES

This sweet treat is great after a nice meal or first thing in the morning. And since the Aeropress offers such flavorful coffee it will stand up to the sweet and creamy white chocolate.

INGREDIENTS:

- 1 tablespoon finely ground coffee
- 1 cup water at 175F
- 2 cups hot milk
- 1/4 teaspoon vanilla extract
- 1/2 cup white chocolate chips
- Whipped cream (optional)

INSTRUCTIONS:

1. Pour the coffee and hot water into the Aeropress chamber and stir for about 10 seconds, then press coffee.
2. In a small sauce pan, heat the milk and add the white chocolate. Stir until the chocolate and milk have combined well.
3. Stir the coffee into the milk mixture and divide into two mugs. Top with whipped cream if desired.

CHAPTER 9
Cappuccinos

Authentic Cappuccino

SERVINGS: 2 | PREP TIME: 10 MINUTES | COOK TIME: 5 MINUTES

This Italian favorite was the first coffee drink to make Americans realize that espresso is an exciting way to prepare coffee. This traditional recipe shows you how to make a cappuccino that will rival anything you've had.

INGREDIENTS:

- 1 tablespoon finely ground coffee
- 1 cup water at 175F
- 1 cup hot milk
- 2 teaspoons sugar
- 1 teaspoon ground cinnamon

INSTRUCTIONS:

1. Pour the coffee and hot water into the Aeropress chamber and stir for about 10 seconds, then press coffee.
2. In a small sauce pan, heat the milk until frothy and nearly boiling.
3. In a blender, combine the coffee, milk, and sugar, and blend on high until frothy.
4. Pour into two cups and top with the ground cinnamon.

Black Forest Cappuccino

SERVINGS: 2 | PREP TIME: 10 MINUTES | COOK TIME: 5 MINUTES

The combination of espresso, chocolate, and cherries gives this drink it's unique appeal. For an interesting after dinner version of this drink, try adding an ounce of brandy or cognac.

INGREDIENTS:

1 tablespoon finely ground coffee
1 cup water at 175F
2 ounces chocolate syrup
2 ounces cherry syrup or cherry puree
1 cup frothed milk
Ground cinnamon for garnish

INSTRUCTIONS:

1. Pour the coffee and hot water into the Aeropress chamber and stir for about 10 seconds, then press coffee.
2. In a small sauce pan, heat the milk and stir in the chocolate syrup and cherry syrup. Stir until the flavors are well combined.
3. Divide the coffee into two mugs and pour in the milk mixture. Spoon some milk foam on top and garnish with the cinnamon.

Cinnamon Mocha Cappuccino

SERVINGS: 2 | PREP TIME: 10 MINUTES | COOK TIME: 5 MINUTES

This take on the classic cappuccino adds a little extra cinnamon, but the big difference comes from a subtle hint of chocolate flavor.

INGREDIENTS:

- 1 tablespoon finely ground coffee
- 1 cup water at 175F
- 1 cup warm milk
- 1 teaspoon ground cinnamon and a little extra for sprinkling on top
- 2 tablespoons chocolate syrup

INSTRUCTIONS:

1. Pour the coffee, hot water, and ground cinnamon into the Aeropress chamber and stir for about 10 seconds, then press coffee.
2. Pour the milk into a microwave safe bowl and microwave on high for about 1 and a half minutes so that the milk is hot but not quite boiling. (This can also be done on the stove)
3. Divide the coffee into two mugs and add one tablespoon of chocolate syrup to each much, stirring well.
4. Pour the steamed milk into each mug. There should be some milk foam that can be spooned on top. Sprinkle on the remaining ground cinnamon and serve.

Hazelnut Cappuccino

SERVINGS: 2 | PREP TIME: 10 MINUTES | COOK TIME: 5 MINUTES

Coffee and hazelnuts are a classic combination, and this recipe will show you how to add hazelnut flavor to robust Aeropress coffee.

INGREDIENTS:

- 1 tablespoon finely ground coffee
- 1 cup water at 175F
- 2 ounces hazelnut syrup
- 1 cup frothed milk
- 2 teaspoons sugar
- Ground cinnamon for garnish

INSTRUCTIONS:

1. Pour the coffee and hot water into the Aeropress chamber and stir for about 10 seconds, then press coffee.
2. In a small sauce pan, heat the milk and whisk until frothy. Then add the hazelnut syrup and sugar to the milk.
3. Divide the coffee into two mugs and pour in the milk.
4. Garnish with the ground cinnamon to serve.

Iced Eggnog Cappuccino

SERVINGS: 2 | PREP TIME: 20 MINUTES | COOK TIME: 5 MINUTES

We've already covered the classic eggnog latte, but this twist on a holiday favorite is great any time you're looking for a rich and playful coffee drink.

INGREDIENTS:

    1 tablespoon finely ground coffee
    1 cup cold water
    2 cups cold milk
    1/2 cup eggnog
    1 teaspoon vanilla extract
    1 teaspoon ground cinnamon
    Ice cubes

INSTRUCTIONS:

1. Pour the coffee, cold water, ground cinnamon, and vanilla extract into the Aeropress chamber and stir for about 10 seconds.
2. Let steep for about 20 minutes, then press coffee.
3. Combine the milk and eggnog and set aside.
4. Fill two glasses with ice and pour in the coffee.
5. Add the milk mixture and stir well before serving.

Mocha Mint Cappuccino

SERVINGS: 2 | PREP TIME: 5 MINUTES | COOK TIME: 5 MINUTES

This non-traditional cappuccino has a fresh hint of mint that will liven up this espresso drink, and a shot of chocolate for a rich and smooth flavor.

INGREDIENTS:

1 tablespoon finely ground coffee
1 cup water at 175F
1 cup hot milk
2 teaspoons peppermint syrup or extract
2 teaspoons chocolate syrup
Ground cinnamon for garnish

INSTRUCTIONS:

1. Pour the coffee and hot water into the Aeropress chamber and stir for about 10 seconds, then press coffee.
2. In a small sauce pan, heat the milk and add the peppermint syrup and chocolate syrup. Heat and whisk until the milk becomes frothy.
3. Divide the coffee into two cups and pour in the milk mixture. Spoon some of the milk foam on top.
4. Garnish with a dash of ground cinnamon on each cup and serve.

CHAPTER 10
Chocolate Caramel Coffees

Amaretto and Chocolate Coffee

SERVINGS: 2 | PREP TIME: 5 MINUTES | COOK TIME: 5 MINUTES

This Italian inspired coffee drink blends sweet almond flavors with chocolate for a complex and rich coffee that will impress your guests or work as a relaxing nightcap.

INGREDIENTS:

- 1 tablespoon finely ground coffee
- 2 cups water at 175F
- 4 tablespoons amaretto almond liqueur
- 2 tablespoons crème de cacao
- Whipped cream (optional)

INSTRUCTIONS:

1. Pour the coffee and half of the hot water into the Aeropress chamber and stir for about 10 seconds, then press coffee.
2. Dilute the coffee with the other cup of hot water.
3. Pour the Amaretto and crème de cacao into two mugs, then add the coffee.
4. Top with whipped cream if desired, and serve immediately.

Black Magic Chocolate Coffee

SERVINGS: 1 | PREP TIME: 5 MINUTES | COOK TIME: 3 MINUTES

The complex flavors in this coffee are just as good for dessert as they are first thing in the morning. And because you're brewing using extracts you don't have to worry about lots of extra calories.

INGREDIENTS:

1 tablespoon ground coffee
2 cups water at 175F
1/4 teaspoon chocolate extract
1/4 teaspoon hazelnut extract
1/4 teaspoon dark rum
1/2 teaspoon sugar or agave syrup
1 tablespoon half and half (optional)

INSTRUCTIONS:

1. Pour the ground coffee, chocolate extract, hazelnut extract, rum, and sugar into the chamber.
2. Add 1 cup of the hot water and stir for about 10 seconds, then press coffee.
3. Remove the Aeropress and dilute the coffee using the other cup of hot water. Stir in the half and half if desired and enjoy.

Brown Sugar Caramel Latte

SERVINGS: 2 | PREP TIME: 10 MINUTES | COOK TIME: 5 MINUTES

This decadent treat is perfect for dessert or entertaining. And since the Aeropress brews rich robust coffee, it will stay perfectly balanced with the other flavors.

INGREDIENTS:

- 1 tablespoon finely ground coffee
- 1 cup water at 175F
- 2 tablespoons brown sugar
- 1/2 cup half and half
- 2 tablespoons caramel sauce

INSTRUCTIONS:

1. Pour the ground coffee and hot water into the Aeropress chamber and stir for 10 seconds, then press coffee.
2. Once the coffee is brewed, stir the brown sugar into the half and half until it is dissolved and a little frothy.
3. Divide the coffee into two mugs and stir in the caramel sauce.
4. Pour one half of the half and half mixture into each coffee mug and stir.

Caramel Macchiato

SERVINGS: 2 | PREP TIME: 20 MINUTES | COOK TIME: 10 MINUTES

Why spend five bucks on a sweet coffee treat at the coffee shop when you can make it yourself with some help from your Aeropress.

INGREDIENTS:

    1 tablespoon finely ground coffee
    1 cup cold water
    1 cup cold milk
    3 tablespoons caramel syrup
    2 cups ice
    Whipped cream (optional)

INSTRUCTIONS:

1. Pour the ground coffee and water into the Aeropress chamber and stir for about 10 seconds. Then let steep for about 20 minutes, then press coffee.
2. In a blender, combine the coffee, milk, caramel syrup, and ice. Blend well. Serve immediately with whipped cream.

Caramel Macchiato with Homemade Vanilla Syrup

SERVINGS: 2 | PREP TIME: 15 MINUTES | COOK TIME: 5 MINUTES

Let's face it, your favorite coffee spot probably charges an arm and a leg for a blended coffee drink like this. But what if you could make one yourself at home and pocket the money you would have spent.

INGREDIENTS:

1 tablespoon finely ground coffee
1 cup water at 175F
4 tablespoons vanilla syrup
2 cups frothed milk
2 tablespoons caramel sauce
Whipped cream
For the Vanilla syrup:
2 cups warm water
2 cups sugar
2 teaspoons vanilla extract

INSTRUCTIONS:

1. Pour the coffee and hot water into the Aeropress chamber and stir for about 10 seconds, then press coffee.
2. Now let's make the vanilla syrup. In a small sauce pan combine the 2 cups of warm water with the sugar. Stir until all of the sugar is dissolved. Remove from heat and add the vanilla extract.
3. Divide the coffee into two mugs and add the vanilla syrup, and frothed milk. Stir well and top with whipped cream.
4. Drizzle one tablespoon of the caramel sauce over the whipped cream and serve.

Chocolate and Vanilla Latte

SERVINGS: 2 | | PREP TIME: 5 MINS | COOK TIME: 3 MINS

A fun twist on the classic flavored latte, this ice cream shop inspired drink will satisfy your craving for hot chocolate and coffee.

INGREDIENTS:

- 2 tablespoons ground coffee
- 1 tablespoon instant cocoa mix
- 1 tablespoon vanilla flavored coffee creamer
- 1/2 teaspoon ground cinnamon
- 2 cups hot milk
- 1 cups water at 175F/79C

INSTRUCTIONS:

1. Pour the ground coffee, cocoa mix, vanilla flavored creamer, and cinnamon into the chamber.
2. Pour the hot water into the chamber and stir for about 30 seconds, then press coffee.
3. Divide the concentrated coffee into two mugs and pour in the hot milk.

Mayan Coffee

SERVINGS: 4 | PREP TIME: 10 MINUTES | COOK TIME: 5 MINUTES

This rich coffee gets its flavor from a combination of spices and extracts that blend to combine a delicious and punchy cup of coffee.

INGREDIENTS:

- 2 tablespoons finely ground coffee
- 2 cups water at 175F
- 2 tablespoons Mexican chocolate
- 4 cups hot milk
- 4 tablespoons sugar
- 1/2 teaspoon vanilla extract
- 1/2 teaspoon almond extract
- 1/2 teaspoon cinnamon
- 1/4 teaspoon cayenne pepper
- Whipped cream (optional)

INSTRUCTIONS:

1. Pour the coffee and half of the hot water into the Aeropress chamber and stir for about 10 seconds, then press coffee.
2. In a small sauce pan, heat the milk and add the sugar, vanilla extract, almond extract, cinnamon, and cayenne pepper until the milk starts to froth.
3. Divide the coffee into four mugs and pour the milk mixture into each mug. Top with whipped cream and serve immediately.

Viennese Coffee

SERVINGS: 2 | PREP TIME: 5 MINUTES | COOK TIME: 35 MINUTES

This old fashioned favorite gets its signature flavor from a combination of chocolate and crème de cacao for an elegant and delicious cup of coffee.

INGREDIENTS:

- 1 tablespoon finely ground coffee
- 2 cups water at 175F
- 2 tablespoons chocolate syrup
- 1 tablespoon sugar
- 1/4 cup crème de cacao
- 1/2 cup heavy whipping cream

INSTRUCTIONS:

1. Pour the coffee and half of the hot water into the Aeropress chamber and stir for about 10 seconds, then press coffee.
2. Dilute the coffee with the other cup of hot water, and in a medium sauce pan combine the coffee, chocolate syrup and sugar. Cook over low heat for 20 min.
3. Add the heavy cream and crème de cacao and cook an additional 10 minutes. Divide coffee into two mugs and serve immediately.

Whipped Chocolate and Vanilla Mocha

SERVINGS: 2 | PREP TIME: 20 MINUTES | COOK TIME: 5 MINUTES

Chocolate and vanilla are both great additions to coffee so why choose only one? This recipe shows you how to use both flavors to create a fun blended coffee drink that will satisfy every taste.

INGREDIENTS:

- 1 tablespoon finely ground coffee
- 1 cup cold water
- 2 cups cold milk or half and half
- 2 tablespoons chocolate syrup
- 1 teaspoon vanilla extract
- 1 cup ice cubes
- Whipped cream (optional)

INSTRUCTIONS:

1. Pour the coffee and cold water into the Aeropress chamber and stir for about 10 seconds. Let steep for about 20 minutes, then press coffee.
2. In a blender, combine the coffee, chocolate syrup, vanilla extract, milk, and ice. Blend until smooth.
3. Pour into two chilled glasses and top with whipped cream.

CHAPTER 11
Mocha Coffees

Caramel Cream Mocha

SERVINGS: 4 | PREP TIME: 10 MINUTES | COOK TIME: 10 MINUTES

This recipe goes heavy on the cream to achieve the richest, most decadent mocha you've ever had.

INGREDIENTS:

- 2 tablespoons finely ground coffee
- 2 cups water at 175F
- 1/2 cup heavy whipping cream
- 1 tablespoon sugar
- 1 teaspoon vanilla extract
- 1/4 cup cocoa powder
- 2 cups half and half
- 1/2 cup caramel syrup
- Whipped cream (optional)

INSTRUCTIONS:

1. Pour the coffee and hot water into the Aeropress chamber and stir for about 10 seconds, then press coffee.
2. In a saucepan, combine the coffee, sugar, vanilla, cocoa powder, half and half, and caramel syrup. Heat until the mixture becomes frothy and slightly thickened.
3. Remove from heat and divide into four mugs, top with whipped cream and serve immediately.

Easy Cinnamon Mocha Latte

SERVINGS: 1 | PREP TIME: 5 MINUTES | COOK TIME: 5 MINUTES

This recipe is so simple that you could make it in the morning before heading to work and skip the stop at the expensive coffee place. And thanks to your Aeropress it's sure to be just as good, if not better.

INGREDIENTS:

- 1 tablespoon finely ground coffee
- 1 cup water at 175F
- 1 cup milk
- 1/4 teaspoon ground cinnamon
- 2 teaspoons cocoa powder

INSTRUCTIONS:

1. Pour the coffee, hot water, and ground cinnamon into the Aeropress chamber and stir for about 10 seconds, then press coffee.
2. In a small sauce pan, heat the milk over medium heat and add the cocoa powder. When the milk is becoming frothy remove from heat and pour into the mug with the coffee. Stir and enjoy.

Hot Cocoa Mocha Latte

SERVINGS: 2 | PREP TIME: 20 MINUTES | COOK TIME: 5 MINUTES

This decadent coffee treat is half hot cocoa and half latte, and thanks to the Aeropress you won't lose the assertive flavor of your favorite coffee beans.

INGREDIENTS:

 1 tablespoon finely ground coffee
 1 cold water
 1 package hot cocoa mix
 2/3 cups almond milk
 2 tablespoons chocolate syrup
 Ice cubes
 Whipped cream (optional)

INSTRUCTIONS:

1. Pour the coffee into the Aeropress chamber with the hot water and stir for about 10 seconds. Then allow coffee to steep for 20 minutes, then press coffee.
2. Put ice into two mugs or glasses.
3. Divide the coffee equally among the two mugs and stir in half of the hot cocoa mix, almond milk, and chocolate syrup. Top with whipped cream if desired.

Mint Mocha Latte

SERVINGS: 2 | PREP TIME: 10 MINUTES | COOK TIME: 5 MINUTES

This recipe shows you a simple way to make a warm, comforting treat that can be enjoyed during the holidays or any time of year.

INGREDIENTS:

- 1 tablespoon finely ground coffee
- 1 cup water at 175F
- 2 cups frothed milk
- 2 tablespoons peppermint syrup
- 2 tablespoons chocolate syrup
- Whipped cream (optional)

INSTRUCTIONS:

1. Pour the coffee and hot water into the Aeropress chamber and stir for about 10 seconds, then press coffee.
2. In a small saucepan heat the milk and add the peppermint syrup and chocolate syrup. Stir until frothed.
3. Divide the coffee into two mugs and add the frothed milk. Stir well and top with whipped cream if desired.

Peanut Butter Mocha

SERVINGS: 2 | PREP TIME: 5 MINUTES | COOK TIME: 5 MINUTES

This fun treat combines coffee, peanut butter and chocolate for a truly decadent coffee experience. And best of all, it's super easy to make.

INGREDIENTS:

- 1 tablespoon finely ground coffee
- 2 cups water at 175F
- 1 packet hot chocolate mix
- 1 cup milk
- 2 tablespoons creamy peanut butter
- 2 cups vanilla ice cream
- Whipped cream (optional)

INSTRUCTIONS:

1. Pour the coffee and half of the hot water into the Aeropress chamber and stir for about 10 seconds, then press coffee.
2. Dilute the coffee with the other cup of hot water.
3. In a blender, combine the coffee, hot chocolate mix, milk, peanut butter, and ice cream, and blend until smooth.
4. Divide into two mugs or glasses and top with whipped cream if desired.

Peppermint Mocha

SERVINGS: 2 | PREP TIME: 5 MINUTES | COOK TIME: 5 MINUTES

Another holiday favorite, the peppermint mocha is a relaxing treat on a cold day. And thanks to your Aeropress the coffee flavor will really shine through.

INGREDIENTS:

- 1 tablespoon finely ground coffee
- 1 cup water at 175F
- 1 package hot cocoa mix
- 1 cup frothed milk
- 2 tablespoons peppermint syrup
- Whipped cream (optional)

INSTRUCTIONS:

1. Pour the coffee and hot water into the Aeropress chamber and stir for about 10 seconds, then press coffee.
2. Heat the milk and whisk to froth and add the hot cocoa mix.
3. Divide the coffee into two mugs and add the peppermint syrup and milk. Top with whipped cream if desired.

Salted Caramel Mocha Frappuccino

SERVINGS: 2 | PREP TIME: 10 MINUTES | COOK TIME: 5 MINUTES

This is the type of coffee drink that often goes for over five bucks at fancy coffee shops, but thanks to this simple recipe, now you can make this treat in your own kitchen.

INGREDIENTS:

- 1 tablespoon finely ground coffee
- 1 cup water at 175F
- 2 tablespoons caramel syrup
- 1 teaspoon sea salt
- 2 tablespoons chocolate syrup
- 1 cup ice cubes
- Whipped cream (optional)

INSTRUCTIONS:

1. Pour the coffee and hot water into the Aeropress chamber and stir for about 10 seconds, then press coffee.
2. In a blender, combine the ice cubes, caramel syrup, sea salt, chocolate syrup, and coffee. Blend well and divide into two glasses. Top with whipped cream if desired.

Simple Cafe Mocha

SERVINGS: 2 | PREP TIME: 10 MINUTES | COOK TIME: 5 MINUTES

Rich, comforting, and simple to make. This take on the classic mocha can be made in minutes thanks to your Aeropress.

INGREDIENTS:

    1 tablespoon finely ground coffee
    1 cup water at 175F
    1 tablespoon cocoa powder
    2 tablespoons sugar
    2 cups milk
    1 teaspoon vanilla extract

INSTRUCTIONS:

1. Pour the coffee, hot water, and vanilla extract into the Aeropress chamber and stir for about 10 seconds, then press coffee.
2. In a small sauce pan, combine the milk, cocoa powder, and sugar over medium heat. Stir until sugar is completely dissolved and the milk is getting frothy.
3. Divide the coffee into two mugs and pour in the milk mixture. Stir well and serve.

CHAPTER 12
Fruity and Spiced Coffees

Banana Coconut Coffee Frappe

SERVINGS: 2 | PREP TIME: 30 MINUTES | COOK TIME: 5 MINUTES

This Hawaiian influenced coffee drink combines the earthy flavor of toasted coconut with banana and cold brewed coffee for a refreshing and sweet treat that is great any time of day.

INGREDIENTS:

- 1 tablespoon finely ground coffee
- 1 cup cold water
- 1 banana, frozen and sliced
- 1 cup coconut milk
- 1 teaspoon vanilla extract
- 1 cup ice cubes

INSTRUCTIONS:

1. Pour the coffee and cold water into the Aeropress chamber and stir for about 10 seconds. Let steep for about 20 minutes, then press coffee.
2. In a blender, combine the coffee, banana, coconut milk, vanilla, and ice cubes. Blend until smooth and pour into two tall glasses.

Berry Mocha

SERVINGS: 4 | PREP TIME: 5 MINUTES | COOK TIME: 10 MINUTES

This mocha recipe combines chocolate with the flavors of three different berries to create a sweet and complex drink that will impress your guests after dinner.

INGREDIENTS:

- 2 tablespoons finely ground coffee
- 2 cups water at 175F
- 2 cups hot milk
- 2 tablespoons hot cocoa mix
- 2 tablespoons strawberry syrups
- 2 tablespoons raspberry syrup
- 2 tablespoons blueberry syrup
- Whipped cream (optional)

INSTRUCTIONS:

1. Pour the coffee and half of the hot water into the Aeropress chamber and stir for about 10 seconds, then press coffee.
2. In a small sauce pan, heat the milk and add the hot cocoa powder, and berry syrups. Heat until the milk becomes frothy.
3. Divide the coffee into four mugs and dilute with the remaining water.
4. Pour the milk mixture evenly into all four mugs, stir, and top with whipped cream to serve.

Blueberry White Chocolate Latte

SERVINGS: 2 | PREP TIME: 5 MINUTES | COOK TIME: 5 MINUTES

The recipe combines subtle hints of fruit and white chocolate to add something different to your usual cup of coffee. Since the Aeropress brews coffee that never has the bitterness or acidity that most coffee does, the other flavors really get a chance to shine.

INGREDIENTS:

- 2 tablespoons finely ground coffee
- 1 cup water at 175F
- 2 cups hot milk
- 2 tablespoons white chocolate sauce
- 2 tablespoons blueberry syrup
- Whipped cream to garnish
- Ground cinnamon to garnish

INSTRUCTIONS:

1. Pour the coffee and hot water into the Aeropress chamber and stir for about 10 seconds, then press coffee.
2. In a small sauce pan, heat the milk and add the white chocolate sauce and blueberry syrup. Stir until milk becomes frothy.
3. Divide the espresso into two mugs and pour half of the milk into each one. Top with whipped cream and a dash of cinnamon to garnish.

Chocolate-Cherry Frappe

SERVINGS: 2 | PREP TIME: 10 MINUTES | COOK TIME: 5 MINUTES

This deeply flavorful coffee drink is part milkshake to satisfy your sweet tooth, but still packs rich coffee flavor thanks to the strong brew from your Aeropress.

INGREDIENTS:

1 tablespoon finely ground coffee
1 cup water at 175F
1/2 cup coconut milk
1/2 cup frozen cherries
1 teaspoon cocoa powder
1 tablespoon sugar
2 cups ice cubes
Whipped cream (optional)

INSTRUCTIONS:

1. Pour the coffee and hot water into the Aeropress chamber and stir for about 10 seconds, then press coffee.
2. Pour the coffee over 1 cup of iced cubes to dilute and cool the coffee.
3. In a blender combine the coffee, remaining ice, cherries, cocoa powder, coconut milk, and sugar. Blend until the cherries have broken down completely and there are no chunks.
4. Divide into two glasses and top with whipped cream if desired.

Coconut Oil Coffee

SERVINGS: 2 | PREP TIME: 5 MINUTES | COOK TIME: 5 MINUTES

For sustained energy and rich flavor this strong cup of coffee can't be beat. And the subtle hint of coconut flavor will nicely compliment the flavor of your Aeropress coffee.

INGREDIENTS:

- 1 tablespoon finely ground coffee
- 2 cups water at 175F
- 2 tablespoons coconut oil
- 2 tablespoons unsalted butter
- 2 tablespoons half and half (optional)

INSTRUCTIONS:

1. Pour the coffee and half of the hot water into the Aeropress chamber and stir for about 10 seconds, then press coffee.
2. In a blender combine the coffee, remaining water, coconut oil, and butter. Blend until smooth and all components are incorporated.
3. Pour into two mugs and, for a slightly less intense flavor try adding a tablespoon of half and half.

Honey Coffee

SERVINGS: 2 | PREP TIME: 5 MINUTES | COOK TIME: 10 MINUTES

This rich cup of coffee achieves a depth of flavor due to a combination of different spices and sweet honey.

INGREDIENTS:

1 tablespoon finely ground coffee
2 cups water at 175F
1/2 cup milk
1/4 cup honey
1/4 teaspoon ground cinnamon
1/8 teaspoon ground nutmeg
1/4 teaspoon vanilla extract

INSTRUCTIONS:

1. Pour the coffee, half of the hot water, cinnamon, and nutmeg into the Aeropress chamber and stir for about 10 seconds, then press coffee.
2. In a saucepan, combine the coffee, remaining water, milk, and honey and heat on medium until well blended.
3. Remove from the heat and add the vanilla. Divide into two mugs and serve immediately.

Raspberry Frappe

SERVINGS: 2 | PREP TIME: 20 MINUTES | COOK TIME: 5 MINUTES

This fruit infused treat is great as a dessert coffee or as a fun way to start the day. The raspberry flavor pairs especially well with the robust flavor of Aeropress coffee.

INGREDIENTS:

- 1 tablespoon finely ground coffee
- 1 cup cold water
- 1 cup half and half or whole milk
- 1/4 cup raspberry syrup
- 3 cups coffee ice cream
- 2 cups ice cubes
- Whipped cream (optional)

INSTRUCTIONS:

1. Pour the coffee and water into the Aeropress chamber and stir for about 10 seconds. Then let steep for about 20 minutes, then press coffee.
2. In a blender combine the coffee, milk, raspberry syrup, ice cream, and ice, and blend until roughly mixed.
3. Pour into tall cold glasses and top with whipped cream if desired.
4. Spiked Cherry Cola

Cold Brew

SERVINGS: 4 | PREP TIME: 25 MINUTES | COOK TIME: 5 MINUTES

This unusual cocktail combines lots of flavors that add up to a well-balanced coffee concoction.

INGREDIENTS:

- 2 tablespoons finely ground coffee
- 2 cups cold water
- 1 (12-ounce) can cherry cola
- 6 ounces vodka or white rum
- Lime wedges for garnish

INSTRUCTIONS:

1. Pour the coffee and half of the cold water into the Aeropress chamber and stir for about 10 seconds. Let steep for about 20 minutes, then press coffee.
2. In a pitcher, combine the coffee, remaining water, cherry cola, and vodka or rum. Stir well and pour into four glasses with ice. Garnish with a lime wedge.

Strawberry Iced Coffee

SERVINGS: 4 | PREP TIME: 20 MINUTES | COOK TIME: 5 MINUTES

Sweet fruit flavors are blended with rich cold brewed Aeropress coffee to create this refreshing summer beverage.

INGREDIENTS:

    2 tablespoons finely ground coffee
    2 cups cold water
    1/3 cup sugar
    1 cup cold milk
    Strawberry syrup
    Ice cubes
    Whipped cream

INSTRUCTIONS:

1. Pour the coffee and cold water into the Aeropress chamber and stir for about 10 seconds. Let steep for about 20 minutes, then press coffee.
2. In a small sauce pan, heat the milk and add the sugar and strawberry syrup, stirring until the sugar is dissolved.
3. Fill four glasses with ice and pour in the coffee. Add the milk mixture and stir.
4. Top with whipped cream and serve.

CHAPTER 13
Iced Coffees

Blended Iced Espresso

SERVINGS: 2 | PREP TIME: 20 MINUTES | COOK TIME: 5 MINUTES

This simple favorite can be made easily at home with the help of your Aeropress and blender. For a mocha flavored drink simply add a tablespoon of cocoa powder.

INGREDIENTS:

- 1 tablespoon finely ground coffee
- 1 cup cold water
- 1 cup cold milk
- 1 tablespoon sugar
- 1 cup ice
- Whipped cream (optional)

INSTRUCTIONS:

1. Pour the coffee and cold water into the Aeropress chamber and stir for about 10 seconds. Let steep for about 20 minutes, then press coffee.
2. In a blender, combine the coffee, milk, sugar, and ice. Blend until smooth and pour into two mugs or glasses. Top with whipped cream to serve.

Caribbean Spiced Coffee Soda

SERVINGS: 4 | PREP TIME: 20 MINUTES | COOK TIME: 5 MINUTES

This island inspired drink is part coffee, part cocktail, part soda, but it is 100% delicious and surprisingly easy to make.

INGREDIENTS:

- 2 tablespoons finely ground coffee
- 2 cups cold water
- 4 ounces Kahlua
- 4 ounces spiced rum
- 1 (12-ounce) bottle or can of cola
- 1/2 cup half and half

INSTRUCTIONS:

1. Pour the coffee and half of the cold water into the Aeropress chamber and stir for about 10 seconds. Let steep for about 20 minutes, then press coffee.
2. In a pitcher, combine the coffee, remaining water, Kahlua, rum, cola, and half and half. Stir well.
3. Fill 4 glasses with ice and pour in the coffee mixture.

Chocolate-Cinnamon Iced Cappuccino

SERVINGS: 1 | PREP TIME: 10 MINUTES | COOK TIME: 5 MINUTES

This recipe brings together the rich flavors of chocolate and cinnamon to create a rich dessert coffee that is complex and satisfying.

INGREDIENTS:

    1 tablespoon finely ground coffee
    1 cup water at 175F
    1/4 cup sweetened condensed milk
    2 tablespoons chocolate syrup
    1/4 teaspoon vanilla extract
    1/4 teaspoon ground cinnamon
    1 cup ice cubes
    Whipped cream (optional)

INSTRUCTIONS:

1. Pour coffee, hot water, and cinnamon into the Aeropress chamber and stir for about 10 seconds, then press coffee.
2. In a blender combine the coffee, condensed milk, chocolate syrup, vanilla extract, and ice cubes. Blend until smooth.
3. Top with whipped cream and serve.

Coconut Mocha Iced Coffee

SERVINGS: 2 | PREP TIME: 20 MINUTES | COOK TIME: 5 MINUTES

The subtle flavor of coconut can enhance a refreshing glass of iced coffee.

INGREDIENTS:

1 tablespoon finely ground coffee
1 cup cold water
1/2 cup coconut milk
2 tablespoons chocolate syrup
1 teaspoon vanilla extract
1 teaspoon sugar
Ice

INSTRUCTIONS:

1. Pour coffee and cold water into the Aeropress chamber and stir for about 10 seconds. Then allow to steep for about 20 minutes, then press coffee.
2. In a blender, combine the coffee, coconut milk, chocolate syrup, vanilla, and sugar. Blend until smooth.
3. Pour over ice to serve.

Coffee Ice Cubes

SERVINGS: 12 | PREP TIME: 5 MINUTES | COOK TIME: 5 MINUTES

If you're looking for the best way to keep your iced coffee drinks for becoming weak and watery this is the perfect solution.

INGREDIENTS:

- 1 tablespoon finely ground coffee
- 1 cup water at 175F
- 1/2 cup cold water
- 1/2 cup cold milk (optional)

INSTRUCTIONS:

1. Pour the coffee and hot water into the Aeropress chamber and stir for about 10 seconds, then press coffee.
2. Dilute the coffee with the cold water.
3. Pour the coffee into an ice cube tray and freeze for at least one hour.
4. You can also try adding 1/2 cup of cold milk to the coffee before freezing.

Cold Brewed Horchata Coffee

SERVINGS: 4 | PREP TIME: 8 HOURS | COOK TIME: 10 MINUTES

This recipe shows you how to combine espresso with horchata to make a creamy spiced Mexican inspired drink, but it'll also show you how to make great horchata from scratch.

INGREDIENTS:

- 2 tablespoons finely ground coffee
- 2 cups cold water
- For the Horchata:
- 8 tablespoons rice
- 1 cup unsalted raw almonds
- 1 teaspoon ground cinnamon
- 6 cups warm water
- 1 cup sugar
- 1 teaspoon vanilla extract, preferably Mexican vanilla

INSTRUCTIONS:

1. Place the rice in a blender and blend well until the rice is powdered. In a large bowl, combine the rice, almonds, cinnamon, and water. Let stand about seven and a half hours.
2. Pour the mixture into a blender and blend until smooth. Strain several times, until there are no solids in the horchata.
3. Pour the horchata into a pitcher and add the sugar and vanilla stirring until the sugar dissolves.
4. Pour the coffee and cold water into the Aeropress chamber and stir for about 10 seconds, then press coffee.
5. Fill four glasses with ice and add the coffee. Pour some horchata into each glass and stir.

Cold Brewed Iced Mocha

SERVINGS: 4 | PREP TIME: 20 MINUTES | COOK TIME: 5 MINUTES

Now we're going to try cold brewing for the most robust iced coffee you've ever had. This recipe is enhanced with some chocolate syrup for a sweet twist.

INGREDIENTS:

- 2 tablespoons finely ground coffee
- 2 cups cold water
- 4 cups cold milk
- 4 tablespoons chocolate syrup
- 4 tablespoons sugar or agave syrup
- Ice

INSTRUCTIONS:

1. Pour in the ground coffee and cold water. Stir well and allow to steep for 20 minutes, then press coffee.
2. Remove the Aeropress and divide the concentrated coffee among 4 glasses with ice.
3. In each of the mugs, mix in one half cup of the milk, and one tablespoon each of the chocolate syrup and sugar. Stir and enjoy.

Cold Brewed Vanilla Caramel Coffee

SERVINGS: 4 | PREP TIME: 25 MINUTES | COOK TIME: 5 MINUTES

This is a great dessert treat or just a fun way of serving coffee on a warm day.

INGREDIENTS:

- 2 tablespoons ground coffee
- 4 cups cold water
- 1 cup cold milk
- 1 teaspoon vanilla extract
- 1/3 cup caramel ice cream topping
- Crushed ice
- Whipped cream (optional)

INSTRUCTIONS:

1. Pour ground coffee into Aeropress chamber with 2 of the cups of cold water, and vanilla extract. Stir and allow to steep for 20 minutes. Press coffee.
2. Pour the concentrated coffee, remaining water, milk, and caramel sauce into a blender with about two cups of crushed ice. Blend well and divide evenly among 4 glasses.
3. Serve with whipped cream if desired.

Frozen Caramel-Cinnamon Latte

SERVINGS: 2 | PREP TIME: 20 MINUTES | COOK TIME: 5 MINUTES

This delightful and sweet coffee frappe combines fresh ground cinnamon with creamy caramel for a fun alternative to a traditional iced coffee

---

INGREDIENTS:

- 1 tablespoon finely ground coffee
- 1 cups cold water
- 4 tablespoons caramel syrup
- 1/2 teaspoon ground cinnamon
- 2 cups cold milk
- 1 teaspoon vanilla extract
- 1 cup ice cubes
- 1/4 teaspoon sea salt
- Whipped cream (optional)

INSTRUCTIONS:

1. Pour the coffee, cold water, and cinnamon into the Aeropress chamber and stir for about 10 seconds. Let steep for about 20 minutes, then press coffee.
2. In a blender, combine the coffee, milk, caramel syrup, vanilla extract, ice, and sea salt. Blend until smooth.
3. Divide into two tall glasses and top with whipped cream to serve.

Hazelnut Mocha Smoothie

SERVINGS: 2 | PREP TIME: 10 MINUTES | COOK TIME: 5 MINUTES

The rich nutty flavor or Nutella improves almost everything. This coffee milkshake is no exception. It's a great way to combine coffee and dessert into one easy dish.

INGREDIENTS:

1 tablespoon finely ground coffee
1 cup water at 175F
1 cup cold milk
1/2 cup Nutella
1 cup ice
2 cups vanilla or coffee ice cream
Whipped cream (optional)

INSTRUCTIONS:

1. Pour the coffee and hot water into the Aeropress chamber and stir for about 10 seconds, then press coffee.
2. Pour the coffee over the ice to cool.
3. In a blender combine the cold coffee with the ice, milk, Nutella, and Vanilla ice cream. Blend until smooth and divide into two tall glasses.
4. Top with whipped cream if desired.

Honey Cinnamon Iced Coffee

SERVINGS: 2 | PREP TIME: 25 MINUTES | COOK TIME: 5 MINUTES

This sweet and spicy iced coffee uses honey for an earthier sweetness than sugar. This allows the natural coffee flavor to really shine through. This coffee can also be served hot.

INGREDIENTS:

- 1 tablespoon finely ground coffee
- 2 cups cold water
- 2 tablespoons honey
- 1 teaspoon ground cinnamon
- 1 cup cold milk

INSTRUCTIONS:

1. Pour the coffee, ground cinnamon, and cold water into the Aeropress chamber and stir for about 10 seconds. Let steep for about 20 minutes, then press coffee.
2. In a blender combine the coffee, honey, remaining water, and milk. Blend until smooth.
3. Fill two glasses with ice and pour in the coffee mixture.

Iced Coconut Latte

SERVINGS: 2 | PREP TIME: 20 MINUTES | COOK TIME: 10 MINUTES

This island inspired drink combines the sweetness of real coconut milk with the rich, bold flavor of Aeropress coffee and just a hint of caramel. This recipe shows you how to serve it cold, but it can also be made as a hot latte as well.

INGREDIENTS:

- 1 tablespoon finely ground coffee
- 1 cups cold water
- 2 tablespoons coconut milk
- 2 tablespoons caramel syrup
- 2 cups cold milk
- 1 cup ice cubes

INSTRUCTIONS:

1. Pour the coffee and water into the Aeropress chamber and stir for about 10 seconds. Let steep for about 20 minutes, then press coffee.
2. Add the coconut milk and caramel syrup to the cold milk and stir.
3. Fill two glasses with ice and pour in the coffee. Then add half of the milk mixture to each glass. Stir well and serve.

Old Fashioned Coffee Soda

SERVINGS: 2 | PREP TIME: 25 MINUTES | COOK TIME: 5 MINUTES

This traditional recipe relies of double strength cold brewed coffee to create a fizzy coffee soda. Feel free to try adding other flavors like caramel or berry to customize this simple beverage.

INGREDIENTS:

- 1 tablespoon finely ground coffee
- 1 cup cold water
- 2 cups club soda
- 4 tablespoons half and half
- Ice cubes

INSTRUCTIONS:

1. Pour the coffee and cold water into the Aeropress chamber and stir for about 10 seconds. Let steep for about 20 minutes, then press coffee.
2. Fill two glasses with ice and pour half of the coffee into each glass.
3. Add the half of the club soda to each glass and stir in the half and half. Enjoy!

Simple Coffee Frappe

SERVINGS: 2 | PREP TIME: 10 MINUTES | COOK TIME: 5 MINUTES

This simple treat can be made in a flash and is a great crossover between coffee and dessert. Since it's so easy to make, it's a great impromptu treat for entertaining.

INGREDIENTS:

1 tablespoon finely ground coffee
1 cup water at 175F
1 cup ice
1/2 cup milk
2 cups vanilla ice cream
2 tablespoons sugar
Whipped cream (optional)

INSTRUCTIONS:

1. Pour the coffee and hot water into the Aeropress chamber and stir for about 10 seconds, then press coffee.
2. Pour the coffee over the ice to cool and then pour into a blender with the milk, ice cream, and sugar. Blend until smooth.
3. Divide into two tall glasses and top with whipped cream if desired.

Simple Cold Brewed Coffee

SERVINGS: 4 | PREP TIME: 20 MINUTES | COOK TIME: 5 MINUTES

Icing hot coffee produces watered down coffee, and chilled hot coffee often tastes dull and stale. By far, the best way to make robust cold coffee is cold brewing. Luckily, your Aeropress is designed to make the world's best tasting cold brewed coffee. And unlike other cold brew systems, your Aeropress will do it in a fraction of the time.

INGREDIENTS:

- 1 tablespoon finely ground coffee
- 2 cups cold water
- Half and half (for serving)

INSTRUCTIONS:

1. Pour the coffee and half cold water into the Aeropress chamber and stir for about 10 seconds. Let steep for about 20 minutes, then press coffee.
2. Dilute the coffee with the remaining water and serve with half and half or milk if desired.

CHAPTER 14
International Coffees

African Coffee Punch

SERVINGS: 10 | PREP TIME: 5 MINUTES | COOK TIME: 5 MINUTES

An unusual and exciting drink for your next party, this African inspired punch combines different liquors and coffee to make something truly unexpected.

INGREDIENTS:

- 2 tablespoons finely ground coffee
- 4 cups water at 175F
- 1 bottle brandy
- 1/2 bottle white rum
- 1 pound white sugar

INSTRUCTIONS:

1. Pour the coffee and half of the hot water into the Aeropress chamber and stir for about 10 seconds, then press coffee.
2. Dilute the coffee with the remaining hot water and add the sugar, stirring until it is completely dissolved.
3. In a large bowl, combine the brandy, rum, and coffee. Stir until blended.

Authentic Irish Coffee

SERVINGS: 2 | PREP TIME: 5 MINUTES | COOK TIME: 5 MINUTES

This after dinner coffee has been around for over a hundred year thanks to its delicious and simple combination of flavors. Just remember to enjoy responsibly.

INGREDIENTS:

- 1 tablespoon finely ground coffee
- 2 cups water at 175F
- 1 tablespoon brown sugar
- 6 tablespoons Irish whiskey
- Heavy cream, slightly whipped

INSTRUCTIONS:

1. Pour the coffee and hot water into the Aeropress chamber and stir for about 10 seconds, then press coffee.
2. Divide the coffee into two mugs and add the brown sugar. Stir until the sugar is completely dissolved.
3. Add 3 tablespoons of whiskey to each mug. Whip the heavy cream until it is halfway to stiff whipped cream. Spoon about 4 tablespoons of cream onto each mug and serve immediately.

Brazilian Coffee

SERVINGS: 2 | PREP TIME: 5 MINUTES | COOK TIME: 5 MINUTES

This exotic coffee drink gets its signature flavors from the combinations of different liqueurs for a complex and unusual flavor. Try using liqueurs made from different types of citrus to customize the drink to your tastes.

INGREDIENTS:

- 1 tablespoon finely ground coffee
- 2 cups water at 175F
- 2 ounces brandy
- 2 ounces Limoncello or Gran Marnier
- 2 ounces Kahlua
- 2 teaspoons sugar
- Whipped cream (optional)

INSTRUCTIONS:

1. Pour the coffee and half of the hot water into the Aeropress chamber and stir for about 10 seconds, then press coffee.
2. Divide the coffee into two mugs and dilute with the remaining water.
3. Add half of the brandy, citrus liqueur, Kahlua, and sugar to each mug. Stir well.
4. Serve topped with whipped cream if desired.

Brazilian Coffee Soda

SERVINGS: 2 | PREP TIME: 20 MINUTES | COOK TIME: 5 MINUTES

The combination of cola and coffee creates a fun, fizzy way to sweeten and enjoy the robust flavor of Aeropress coffee. And it's topped off with a little chocolate to add another layer of flavor.

INGREDIENTS:

- 1 tablespoon finely ground coffee
- 1 cup cold water
- 1 (12-ounce) can cola
- 2 cups cold milk
- 2 tablespoons chocolate sauce
- 2 cups vanilla ice cream

INSTRUCTIONS:

1. Pour the coffee and cold water into the Aeropress chamber and stir for about 10 seconds. Let steep for about 20 minutes, then press coffee.
2. Combine the coffee, cola, and chocolate sauce.
3. Scoop the ice cream into two glasses and pour the coffee mixture in. Serve immediately.

Cuban Iced Coffee

SERVINGS: 2 | PREP TIME: 25 MINUTES | COOK TIME: 5 MINUTES

This light refreshing coffee cocktail combines rich coffee flavor with a taste of the islands. A perfect beverage for unwinding after a long day. It's like a mini vacation courtesy of your Aeropress.

INGREDIENTS:

   1 tablespoon finely ground coffee
   2 cups cold water
   1 tablespoon sugar
   4 ounces white rum
   1/2 cup cold milk
   Mint leaves
   Ice cubes

INSTRUCTIONS:

1. Pour the coffee and half of the cold water into the Aeropress chamber and stir for about 10 seconds. Let steep for about 20 minutes, then press coffee.
2. In a tall glass muddle the mint leaves with the sugar and ice. Add rum and stir.
3. Dilute the coffee with the remaining water and pour half into each glass. Stir half of the milk into each glass and garnish with a mint leaf.

Dublin Iced Coffee

SERVINGS: 2 | PREP TIME: 25 MINUTES | COOK TIME: 5 MINUTES

This rich and thick coffee cocktail is well rounded and robust thanks to a wide variety of flavors. This isn't your traditional Irish coffee.

INGREDIENTS:

- 1 tablespoon finely ground coffee
- 1 cup cold water
- 4 ounces dark beer, preferably Guinness
- 3 ounces Irish whiskey
- 1 tablespoon sugar
- 2 tablespoons heavy cream

INSTRUCTIONS:

1. Pour the coffee and cold water into the Aeropress chamber and stir for about 10 seconds. Let steep for about 20 minutes, then press coffee.
2. In two tall glasses stir together the coffee, beer, whiskey and sugar.
3. Add the ice and cream and gently stir.

Guatemalan Hop

SERVINGS: 2 | PREP TIME: 5 MINUTES | COOK TIME: 5 MINUTES

This tasty Central American treat packs a punch thanks to two types of liqueur and the robust flavor of Aeropress coffee. If possible, use Guatemalan coffee to truly appreciate the traditional flavor of this unique drink.

INGREDIENTS:

- 1 tablespoon finely ground coffee (preferably Guatemalan)
- 1 cup water at 175F
- 2 ounces rum
- 2 ounces crème de cacao
- 1 ounce half and half
- Whipped cream (optional)

INSTRUCTIONS:

1. Pour the coffee and hot water into the Aeropress chamber and stir for about 10 seconds, then press coffee.
2. Divide coffee into two mugs and add half of the rum, crème de cacao, and half and half to each mugs. Stir well and serve topped with whipped cream if desired.

Irish Cappuccino

SERVINGS: 4 | PREP TIME: 5 MINUTES | COOK TIME: 5 MINUTES

This crossover of flavors is inspired by traditional coffee recipes from two countries who understand the value of adding a bit of liqueur to coffee. The Irish cream and the Amaretto mix to create a creamy sweetness that is perfect in place of dessert.

INGREDIENTS:

- 2 tablespoons finely ground coffee
- 2 cups water at 175F
- 2 cups hot milk
- 4 ounces Irish cream liqueur
- 4 ounces Amaretto
- 4 teaspoons sugar
- Ground cinnamon to garnish

INSTRUCTIONS:

1. Pour the coffee and half of the hot water into the Aeropress chamber and stir for about 10 seconds, then press coffee.
2. In a small sauce pan, heat the milk over medium heat and add the sugar, stirring until it dissolves. When the milk is frothy and almost boiling add the Irish cream and Amaretto and remove from heat.
3. Divide the coffee into four mugs and pour in the milk. Top with the milk foam and sprinkle on a dash of cinnamon. Serve immediately.

Mexican Espresso

SERVINGS: 1 | PREP TIME: 5 MINUTES | COOK TIME: 5 MINUTES

This twist on traditional Mexican coffee is even stronger and more robust, but thanks to the Aeropress, it will be smooth and creamy and never bitter.

INGREDIENTS:

    1 tablespoon finely ground coffee
    1 cup water at 175F
    1 ounce coffee liqueur such as Kahlua
    1 teaspoon sugar
    Whipped cream (optional)

INSTRUCTIONS:

1. Pour the ground coffee and hot water into the Aeropress chamber and stir for about 10 seconds, then press coffee.
2. Add the coffee liqueur and sugar to the coffee and top with whipped cream to serve.

Spicy Thai Iced Coffee

SERVINGS: 1 | PREP TIME: 5 MINUTES | COOK TIME: 5 MINUTES

Iced coffee with a kick of exotic spices is a great way to enjoy coffee on a summer day. This recipe combines sweets and spices to make a robust and complex treat.

INGREDIENTS:

- 1 tablespoon finely ground coffee
- 1/4 teaspoon ground coriander
- 1 tablespoon ground cardamom
- 1/4 teaspoon ground cinnamon
- 2 tablespoons sweetened condensed milk
- 1 tablespoon heavy cream or half and half
- 1 cups water at 175F
- 1 cup of cold water

INSTRUCTIONS:

1. Pour the coffee grounds, coriander, cardamom, and cinnamon into the chamber and add 1 cup of hot water.
2. Stir the mixture for about 10 seconds and let steep for another minute, then press coffee.
3. Remove the Aeropress and dilute the coffee with the cold water. Then add the cream, condensed milk, and ice. Stir well.

Thai Coffee

SERVINGS: 2 | PREP TIME: 5 MINUTES | COOK TIME: 3 MINUTES

An exotic way to spice up your daily cup of coffee. And thanks to your Aeropress, the delicate flavors will really stand out.

INGREDIENTS:

- 2 tablespoons ground coffee
- 1/4 teaspoon ground cardamom
- 4 cups water at 175F/79C
- 2 tablespoons sweetened condensed milk

INSTRUCTIONS:

1. Pour the coffee grounds and ground cardamom into the chamber.
2. Pour in half of the water and stir for about 10 seconds, then press coffee.
3. Divide the coffee between two mugs and pour one tablespoon of condensed milk into each cup. Stir well and enjoy.

The World's Best Pumpkin Spice Latte

SERVINGS: 2 | PREP TIME: 15 MINUTES | COOK TIME: 10 MINUTES

We had to get around to it eventually... The pumpkin spice latte has become a seasonal phenomenon that cannot be ignored. So here it is, the best pumpkin spice latte you've ever had.

INGREDIENTS:

1 tablespoon finely ground coffee
1 cup water at 175F
2 tablespoons canned pumpkin
1 teaspoon pumpkin spice powder
2 tablespoons sugar
2 teaspoons vanilla extract
2 cups milk
Whipped cream (optional)

INSTRUCTIONS:

1. Pour the coffee and hot water into the Aeropress chamber and stir for about 10 seconds, then press coffee.
2. In a small saucepan combine the canned pumpkin and spices. Stir until well combined.
3. Stir in the sugar and mix until it has the consistency of syrup.
4. Stir in the milk and vanilla extract.
5. Pour the syrup into a blender and add the coffee. Blend on medium for about 15 seconds.
6. Divide into two mugs and top with whipped cream if desired.

Traditional Turkish Coffee

SERVINGS: 1 | PREP TIME: 5 MINUTES | COOK TIME: 5 MINUTES

This strong traditional coffee is similar to espresso but with the addition of spices to add a deep richness to an already robust style of coffee.

INGREDIENTS:

    1 tablespoon finely ground coffee
    1 cup of water at 175F
    1/8 teaspoon ground cardamom
    Sugar (optional)

INSTRUCTIONS:

1. Pour the ground coffee, water and ground cardamom into the chamber, and stir for about 10 seconds. Allow to steep for an additional five minutes, then press coffee.
2. This coffee does not need to be diluted and should be served very strong. At this point add sugar to taste and enjoy.

Vietnamese Coffee

SERVINGS: 2 | PREP TIME: 20 MINUTES | COOK TIME: 5 MINUTES

This strong, sweet traditional Vietnamese coffee is a rich way to start the day or a great after dinner coffee on a hot summer day.

INGREDIENTS:

- 1 tablespoon finely ground coffee
- 2 cups cold water
- 4 tablespoons sweetened condensed milk
- 1 cup half and half or whole milk
- Ice

INSTRUCTIONS:

1. Pour the coffee and cold water into the Aeropress chamber and stir for about 10 seconds. Then let steep for about 20 minutes, then press coffee.
2. Dilute the coffee with the other cup of water and then pour into a tall glass of ice.
3. Pour in the condensed milk and half and half. Stir and enjoy.

Warm Gingerbread Irish Coffee

SERVINGS: 2 | PREP TIME: 5 MINUTES | COOK TIME: 5 MINUTES

This modern update to the traditional Irish coffee is fun and has the feeling of Fall in every sip.

INGREDIENTS:

- 1 tablespoon finely ground coffee
- 1 cup water at 175F
- 4 ounces Irish cream liqueur
- 2 teaspoons pumpkin spice powder
- Ground cinnamon for garnish

INSTRUCTIONS:

1. Pour the coffee, pumpkin spice and hot water into the Aeropress chamber and stir for about 10 seconds, then press coffee.
2. Pour the coffee into two mugs and then add the Irish cream and stir.
3. Garnish with a dash of cinnamon.

CHAPTER 15
Coffee Cocktails

Cafe Imperial

SERVINGS: 2 | PREP TIME: 5 MINUTES | COOK TIME: 5 MINUTES

This French inspired coffee drink is perfect for a chilly night or relaxing after dinner. The Aeropress enhances all of this by creating a rich and creamy base for this sophisticated drink.

INGREDIENTS:

- 1 tablespoon finely ground coffee
- 2 cups water at 175F
- 1 ounce orange liquor such as Gran Marnier
- 1 teaspoon sugar
- Whipped cream (optional)

INSTRUCTIONS:

1. Pour the ground coffee into the Aeropress chamber and add half of the hot water. Stir for 10 seconds, then press coffee.
2. Dive the coffee equally into two mugs and stir in the orange liquor and sugar.
3. Top with whipped cream if desired and serve.

Cafe Rumba

SERVINGS: 4 | PREP TIME: 10 MINUTES | COOK TIME: 5 MINUTES

This island inspired coffee has hints of cinnamon and dark rum for deep rich flavors. It can also be poured over ice for a delicious spiked iced coffee.

INGREDIENTS:

- 2 tablespoons ground coffee
- 4 cups water at 175F
- 1 cup hot milk
- 2 teaspoons vanilla extract
- 4 tablespoons sugar
- 8 tablespoons dark rum
- 1 teaspoon ground cinnamon
- 1 cup heavy whipping cream

INSTRUCTIONS:

1. Pour the coffee, half of the hot water, and ground cinnamon into the Aeropress chamber and stir for about 10 seconds, then press coffee.
2. Dilute the coffee with the remaining 2 cups of water and add the rum.
3. In a bowl whip the cream and add the sugar and vanilla extract. When the whipped cream is stiff, spoon equal amounts into 4 glasses.
4. Pour the coffee over the whipped cream to serve.

Chocolate Stout Affogato

SERVINGS: 2 | PREP TIME: 5 MINUTES | COOK TIME: 5 MINUTES

This Italian combination of espresso, ice cream, and dark beer is as decadent as it gets, and thanks to your Aeropress, you're sure to have the most balanced flavor possible.

INGREDIENTS:

- 1 tablespoon finely ground coffee
- 1 cup water at 175F
- 2 scoops coffee ice cream
- 3 ounces chocolate liqueur
- 1 cup chocolate stout beer

INSTRUCTIONS:

1. Pour the coffee and hot water into the Aeropress chamber and stir for about 10 seconds, then press coffee.
2. Place one scoop of iced cream in two chilled glasses.
3. Pour half of the espresso, chocolate liqueur, and beer into each glass and gently stir. Serve immediately.

Coffee Liqueur

SERVINGS: 24 | PREP TIME: 5 MINUTES | COOK TIME: 15 MINUTES

This recipe will show you how to use your Aeropress coffee to make a flavorful version of a traditional coffee liqueur that can be enjoyed in coffee or any number of other drinks and cocktails.

INGREDIENTS:

- 2 tablespoons finely ground coffee
- 4 cups water at 175F
- 4 cups sugar
- 2 tablespoons vanilla extract
- 4 cups vodka

INSTRUCTIONS:

1. Pour the coffee and half of the hot water into the Aeropress chamber and stir for about 10 seconds, then press coffee.
2. In a medium saucepan, combine the coffee, remaining water, and sugar and bring to a boil. Simmer for about 10 minutes and remove from heat.
3. When the mixture has cooled add the vanilla extract and vodka and stir.
4. Pour the liqueur into bottles or jars to store.

Creamy Cinnamon Coffee Punch

SERVINGS: 12 | PREP TIME: 10 MINUTES | COOK TIME: 5 MINUTES

This creamy treat is perfect for entertaining on a hot summer day. If you'd like to spice things up a bit, try adding your favorite liqueur for a punchier punch.

INGREDIENTS:

- 2 tablespoons finely ground coffee
- 4 cups water at 175F
- 1 teaspoon ground cinnamon
- 1 (12-ounce) can sweetened condensed milk
- 1/2 cup sugar
- 1/2 gallon vanilla ice cream

INSTRUCTIONS:

1. Pour the coffee, 2 cups of hot water, and ground cinnamon into the Aeropress chamber and stir for about 10 seconds, then press coffee.
2. In a bowl, dilute the coffee with the remaining water and stir in the condensed milk, and sugar.
3. Scoop the ice cream into a punch bowl and pour the coffee mixture over it.

Creamy Spiked Coffee

SERVINGS: 2 | PREP TIME: 5 MINUTES | COOK TIME: 5 MINUTES

This coffee drink is loaded with flavor thanks to the combination of Aeropress coffee and a variety of complimentary liqueurs. This is not your morning cup of coffee so enjoy this one responsibly.

INGREDIENTS:

- 1 tablespoon finely ground coffee
- 2 cups water at 175F
- 2 ounces brandy or Irish whiskey
- 2 ounces Irish cream
- 2 ounces vanilla vodka
- 2 ounces cinnamon schnapps

INSTRUCTIONS:

1. Pour the coffee and half of the hot water into the Aeropress chamber and stir for about 10 seconds, then press coffee.
2. Divide the coffee into two mugs and dilute with the remaining water.
3. Add half of the brandy, Irish cream, vodka, and schnapps to each mug, stir well and serve hot.

Spiced Coffee Cocktail

SERVINGS: 4 | PREP TIME: 25 MINUTES | COOK TIME: 10 MINUTES

Handmade cocktails are all the rage right now. Why not use coffee as a base? This recipe shows you how to combine coffee, spices, and a little booze to make an out of this world cocktail.

INGREDIENTS:

- 2 tablespoons finely ground coffee
- 2 cups cold
- 1/4 teaspoon ground cumin
- 1/2 teaspoon ground star anise
- 1/2 teaspoon ground cinnamon plus more for garnish
- 2 teaspoons sugar
- 4 tablespoons half and half
- 8 tablespoons brandy or whiskey

INSTRUCTIONS:

1. Pour the coffee and half of the cold water, cumin, star anise, and cinnamon into the Aeropress chamber and stir for about 10 seconds. Let steep for about 20 minutes, then press coffee.
2. In a small bowl whisk together the half and half, sugar, whiskey and remaining water.
3. Add the coffee to the half and half mixture and stir well.
4. Pour the cocktail into chilled martini glasses and garnish with ground cinnamon.

Summer Espresso Gin Fizz

SERVINGS: 4 | PREP TIME: 25 MINUTES | COOK TIME: 5 MINUTES

This refreshing summer cocktail has a hint of rich coffee to offset the sweet fruit and herbal flavors of the gin to make a nice balanced beverage.

INGREDIENTS:

- 1 tablespoon finely ground coffee
- 1/2 cup cold water
- 6 ounces gin
- 12 blackberries
- 2 ounces simple syrup

INSTRUCTIONS:

1. Pour the coffee and cold water into the Aeropress chamber and stir for about 10 seconds. Let steep for about 20 minutes, then press coffee.
2. In four tumbler glasses muddle the blackberries with the simple syrup.
3. Add one and a half ounces of gin to each glass and stir. Then add two ounces of espresso to each glass and stir again.
4. Sweet and Creamy

Irish Coffee

SERVINGS: 2 | PREP TIME: 5 MINUTES | COOK TIME: 5 MINUTES

This new take on Irish coffee is sweeter and creamier than the traditional recipe, but still packs a punch that makes it a perfect after dinner drink or night cap.

INGREDIENTS:

- 1 tablespoon finely ground coffee
- 2 cups water at 175F
- 3 ounces Irish whiskey
- 2 ounces Irish cream liqueur
- 2 teaspoons light brown sugar
- 2 tablespoons half and half
- Whipped cream (optional)

INSTRUCTIONS:

1. Pour the coffee and hot water into the Aeropress chamber and stir for about 10 seconds, then press coffee.
2. Divide the coffee into two mugs and add half of the whiskey, Irish cream liqueur, brown sugar, and half and half to each mug, and stir until the sugar is dissolved.
3. Top with whipped cream and serve immediately.

The Dude

SERVINGS: 4 | PREP TIME: 25 MINUTES | COOK TIME: 5 MINUTES

Inspired by the titular character from the film The Big Lebowski, this coffee drink combines strong espresso with a White Russian for a whimsical way to entertain the film buffs in your life.

INGREDIENTS:

- 1 tablespoon finely ground coffee
- 2 cups cold water
- 2 cups cold milk
- 8 ounces Kahlua
- 4 ounces vodka
- Ice cubes

INSTRUCTIONS:

1. Pour the coffee and half of the cold water into the Aeropress chamber and stir for about 10 seconds. Let steep for about 20 minutes, then press coffee.
2. In a pitcher, combine the coffee, milk, remaining water, Kahlua, and vodka. Stir well
3. Fill four glasses with ice and pour the mixture.

Warm Strawberry Vanilla Espresso Cocktail

SERVINGS: 2 | PREP TIME: 10 MINUTES | COOK TIME: 5 MINUTES

This sweet espresso treat has just a hint of alcohol to add a little depth to rich coffee and strawberry flavor.

INGREDIENTS:

- 1 tablespoon finely ground coffee
- 1 cup water at 175F
- 2 ounces vanilla vodka
- 1 ounce Frangelico
- Whipped cream (optional)

INSTRUCTIONS:

1. Pour the coffee and hot water into the Aeropress chamber and stir for about 10 seconds, then press coffee.
2. In two mugs stir together the vodka and Frangelico, then add the coffee.
3. Top with whipped cream and serve immediately.

CHAPTER 16
Bonus

Desserts You Can Make with Aeropress Coffee:

Perhaps the reason that coffee is so often served with dessert is because they naturally go together. The rich, earthy flavor of coffee just seems to pair well with a bit of sweetness, making for the perfect end to a great meal. In this section we'll take that one step further and show you how you can make desserts using Aeropress coffee right in the recipe. We're going to feature two classic recipes that put the flavor of espresso right up front. First, let's talk about how to make a classic Italian dessert staple, Tiramisu. The sweetness of the mascarpone cheese is elevated with the introduction of espresso soaked lady fingers for a perfect balance of flavors.

The Perfect Aeropress Tiramisu

SERVINGS: 8 | PREP TIME: 30 MINUTES | COOK TIME: 10 MINUTES

INGREDIENTS:

- 1/4 cup Aeropress espresso
- 6 egg yolks
- 3/4 cups sugar
- 2/3 cups milk
- 1 1/4 cups heavy cream
- 1/2 teaspoon vanilla extract
- 1 pound mascarpone cheese
- 2 tablespoons rum
- 2 packages lady finger cookies
- 1 tablespoon cocoa powder

INSTRUCTIONS:

1. In a medium sauce pan whisk together the egg yolks and sugar. Then add the milk and cook until the mixture reaches a boil. Remove from heat, cover and place in the refrigerator.
2. Using a mixer, beat together the heavy cream and vanilla until it becomes stiff. Then whisk in the mascarpone until thoroughly blended.
3. In another bowl stir together the espresso and rum.
4. Place the lady fingers on a baking sheet and pour the espresso/rum mixture over them and allow to soak.
5. In a baking dish, arrange a layer of the soaked lady fingers on the bottom. Spread enough mascarpone over them to cover, and then add a layer of the whipped cream. Then repeat these steps, starting with another layer of lady fingers.
6. Cover the baking dish and chill in the refrigerator for at least 3 hours before serving.
7. When ready to serve, dust the top with the cocoa powder and serve immediately.

Aeropress Espresso Cheesecake

SERVINGS: 10 | PREP TIME: 30 MINUTES | COOK TIME: 60 MINUTES

Cheesecake is an excellent canvas for creative flavors and this recipe will show you how to use strong Aeropress coffee to make a rich and flavorful cheesecake that is sure to wow your guests.

INGREDIENTS:

For the filling:
- 1/4 cup Aeropress espresso
- 1 tablespoon finely ground coffee
- 1 tablespoon water
- 24 ounces cream cheese
- 1 cup sugar
- 3 eggs
- 1/4 cup unsalted butter, melted

For the Crust:
- 10 ounces chocolate wafers or graham crackers
- 1 stick unsalted butter, melted

INSTRUCTIONS:

1. Preheat oven to 400F.
2. In a food processor, grind the cookies and add the butter. Then press the moist cookie mixture into the bottom of a greased 9-inch pan and set aside.
3. In a bowl, mix the cream cheese until smooth and add the sugar and beat until the mixture becomes fluffy.
4. Add the eggs one at a time and then mix in the espresso, butter and ground coffee.
5. Pour the filling mixture into the crust and bake for about 40 minutes or until the top is golden brown.
6. Remove from the oven and cool on a rack for at least one hour and then place in the refrigerator for twelve hours.

Marinate Meat with Aeropress Coffee

Coffee can be used as a preparation for meat in several different ways. We'll discuss how you can use ground coffee as a rub, or use prepared espresso as part of a marinade to give meat a deep, earthy flavor.

Espresso as a rub:

This one is pretty simple but is often overlooked by grill cooks. This works best with beef, lamb, and pork, but you can try it with anything you plan to cook on the grill. When you're at the seasoning stage, add some finely ground coffee to your salt and pepper mixture and rub all over the meat. When the meat cooks, the heat from the grill will interact with the coffee to create a unique smoky flavor that will enhance the flavor of the meat.

Espresso as a marinade:

There are endless ways to marinate meat, but adding some Aeropress espresso to a traditional marinade you can greatly enhance the flavor of most meats by giving it a deep complex flavor. Here's a great marinade recipe for beef, lamb, or chicken.

INGREDIENTS:

- 1/2 cup Aeropress strong brewed espresso
- 3 tablespoons red wine vinegar
- 2 teaspoons minced garlic
- 1 tablespoon olive oil
- 1 tablespoon rosemary, preferably fresh
- 1 teaspoon sea salt
- 1 teaspoon ground pepper
- 1 tablespoon lemon juice

INSTRUCTIONS:

1. In a large bowl, combine all ingredients and stir well.
2. To use, place your meat in a large plastic storage bag and pour in the marinade. Let the meat marinate for an hour or two before cooking. Don't let the meat marinate longer than three hours or it will affect the texture of the meat.
3. Spice Up Sauces with Aeropress Espresso
4. Adding some Aeropress espresso directly to a sauce can greatly improve its depth of flavor. This traditional barbecue sauce is enhanced with the addition of a little earthy coffee flavor. It can be used on literally anything you're planning to grill or smoke.

INGREDIENTS:

1/2 cup Aeropress espresso
4 tablespoons minced garlic
4 tablespoons olive oil
1 cup apple cider vinegar
1/2 cup soy sauce
2 cups ketchup
2 cups honey
1 tablespoon sea salt

INSTRUCTIONS:

1. Simply mix all the ingredients together and slather on meat before and after cooking for the most flavorful barbecue sauce you've ever had.

ESSENTIAL INGREDIENTS FOR EXCITING COFFEE DRINKS

Choose your perfect roast

Obviously the most important part of coffee is the beans and since there are so many different types of bean, choosing the right ones is important. As we discussed in an earlier chapter, the region and roast really determine the flavor so experiment with some different types and see which you prefer.

Syrups and flavors

At most upscale coffee places, you'll find a wall of different flavored syrups to enhance coffee drinks. Most of these can be purchased in a supermarket. Since you might not have room for them all, some essentials are: caramel syrup, almond, peppermint, and vanilla. With these four flavors you can create a multitude of different concoctions.

Toppings

Many of the drinks we've discussed are topped with whipped cream. But is there really a difference between the whipped cream in a can and the kind you make yourself? The answer is, yes. While the canned whipped cream may be convenient, it doesn't have the firm texture of handmade whipped cream. For warm coffee drinks this is important because the thicker the cream, the better it will stand up to the hot coffee. It may take an extra few minutes, but homemade whipped cream is definitely worth it.

Liqueurs

We've been adding liquor to coffee for a long time, and it's probably because the flavors pair so well together. To become an expert at making spiked coffees, it's a good idea to keep certain alcoholic staples on hand. Probably the most common addition to coffee would be Irish whiskey since the Irish coffee has always been a popular choice. It is also recommended to keep on hand a supply of an Irish cream like Baily's, and some flavored liqueurs such as Kahlua, Gran Marnier, and Framboise. More exotic liqueurs such as Amaretto are also good for making fun and original creations. Of course, you can try whatever flavors you like to make coffee drinks that appeal to your taste, but having these liqueurs standing by will ensure that you can whip up a batch of creative drinks any time.

NEXT STEPS...

DID YOU ENJOY THE BOOK?

IF SO, THEN LET ME KNOW BY LEAVING A REVIEW ON AMAZON! Reviews are the lifeblood of independent authors. I would appreciate even a few words and rating if that's all you have time for.

IF YOU DID NOT LIKE THIS BOOK, THEN PLEASE TELL ME! Email me at feedback@HHFpress.com and let me know what you didn't like! Perhaps I can change it. In today's world a book doesn't have to be stagnant, it can improve with time and feedback from readers like you. You can impact this book, and I welcome your feedback. Help make this book better for everyone!

www.ingramcontent.com/pod-product-compliance
Lightning Source LLC
Chambersburg PA
CBHW050323120526
44592CB00014B/2022